Neil Willis has always been a Buckinghamshire man.
Educated at The Royal Grammar School, High Wycombe,
it is only in his early 50s that he started to write. This book
is a poetry collection about love, life, death and loss.

Thank you to Emma, my wife, for being part of my hundred.

To Adrian Lord, thanks for the inspiration of your wonderful piano music.

And, sadly, to my dearest father, John, whose death started my writing journey.

Neil Willis

ONE YEAR ON
MY HUNDRED

AUSTIN MACAULEY PUBLISHERS™

LONDON * CAMBRIDGE * NEW YORK * SHARJAH

A CIP catalogue record for this title is available from the British Library.

ISBN 9781398402553 (Paperback)
ISBN 9781398402560 (Hardback)
ISBN 9781398402577 (ePub e-Book)

www.austinmacauley.com

First Published (2021)
Austin Macauley Publishers Ltd
25 Canada Square
Canary Wharf
London
E14 5LQ

CONTENTS

Each tear is a reflection of your mind.
Each smile is a sunbeam from your heart.
Every step is part of your life's pathway.
Every hand held helps others on theirs.

Poems of Love

1. Dance of Love

I'm circling with pin toes
In meadows of flowers,
My arms undulate, slow as I turn.
Breathing calmly, I'm feeling for you.

It's my solo dance of love.

Unclenched hands release trails of blossom.

I'm floating in clear skies
To sunsets of colours,
My arms spreading outward as I turn.
Eyes closed, I'm dreaming of us.
It's my solo flight of love.
Reddened clouds vapour streams of passion.

I'm standing on blue shores
In lowing white breakers,
The waves lapping over my ankles.
Head high, arms out, I'm draining sun.
It's my solo stand to love.
Your voice in the wind, hushing through my ears.

I'm sleeping naked in bed
On silken cream pillows.
My body curled as an embryo.
Dreaming calmness brings me to you.
It's my solo dream of love.
Cupped hands to my heart, hold my yearning.

We are dancing in the dark
On trouper-lit floorboards.
Our heads are angled for the tango.
Black silhouettes vogue body to body.
It's our sexual dance of love.
Stocking legs to my thigh, shows your desire.

Darling, will you be my love?

Can you feel my love?

As we spin, will we be dizzy in love?

As you pass into my arms,
Smile ... that look of love.

Everything *I* do, ... is *our* dance of love.

2. We Watched The Sun Rise

We have watched the sun rise
With indecent hair on windswept beaches,
Where the clouds were frowns over brows.
As the eyeball sun peeked through as red
The sands had written their unplayed tune,
Drawn with dried staff lines of seaweed,
While beach jellyfish were musical notes.
Sunbeam fingers plucked the white crests,
And waves were percussion all day long.

We've been humbled by mountains
That cried so hard after the storms fled,
One hundred tears fell to the green glens.
Proud stags looked above ferns to see
A ribbon pinned to the distant hills;
A rainbow badge of remembrance
To the foul rains that were now past,
But also a brightly shining broach
For the fairer weather, in the day ahead.

We have adored the last sun
Set red on the waterline to the sky,
So colouring the river's evening still.
Salmon slept under the darkened weed,
Late swallows darted low for their last meal.
Tall sailing boat masts, that were white lines,
Became silhouettes ... and then darkness,
While halyard hooks clinked in the wind
A lullaby through 'til dawn.

Inveraray rose as a pop-up
In a small child's book, with fairy-tale bridges
Leading to the fabled green castle.
Low mist on the loch was the villain
Creeping behind good ladies and lords.
Late morning sun slayed the Hooded Claw,
Light celebrated amber heather.
While tall white buildings shone alleluia
By storm grey skies and dark blue water.

On Orleans French Quarter streets
Saxophone notes were blues against
Yellow houses, with wooden shutters.
Jazz echoed with a happier beat
That we skipped a step as we walked.
Hear the sugar boat whistle its long note.
Black native music played anthems.
See carnival parades, with necklace beads
Thrown from balconies to those below.

....

We look on ice cream childhoods
Where the many stories to our minds,
Seemed so vivid, they became real.
What I have read is not a fairytale,
Because we have played our own parts;
Dancing through each chapter and verses.
So now is the time to take your hand,
To walk along sparkling champagne shores,
On our ever journey to nirvana.

3. Fingers

"Wow," you said.

You were right, our hands perfectly matched,
As I lay my fingers over yours.
I felt the coolness of your evening skin,
My tips crept along, as though to explore.

You were right. Our eyes brighten lovingly.
God had latched them to almost meld.
Ten digits that tell each other how we're feeling,
When they clasp, they clasp, perfectly held.

Five splayed fingers in the air,
As we kissed, showed true love flared.

Fingers to hold you,
That say I told you,
That say they're sorry,
Or squeeze with worry.
Fingers assure you,
To be there for you,
That give truthful calm
And keep from harm.
When I'm frightened,
They are tightened.
They lead and follow,
To our tomorrows.

But cupped fingers on my chest,
Are love and calm, as we lie to rest.

I wanted to show you the whole of the world.
You were right, we should look to stars.
We should think of our love as a symphony,
Where reams of long-tailed notes contrast.

Just in that moment, our hearts glowed.
You were right. Our love colour we should choose.
We imagined our lives as a kaleidoscope,
Rainbows impassion red, yellow and blues.

You were right. Nothing would ever be wrong,
As I adored you, nose rubbed nose.
Four eyes that gleed the word "forever,"
Infinity was our love number chose.

Just in that moment, our hearts glowed.

4. Snow Morn

And our warm breaths blew condensation straight passed our
frozen red noses ...

Running, running, running,
Running through the snow,
Racing, racing, racing,
Faster than we should go.
Legs of lead,
Soles of rubber,
Our footprints left to show.
It'll snow again tonight.
... And were we ever here ?
Tomorrow wouldn't know !

... And that night,
... It did snow.
... I couldn't sleep.
Under street lights
Cotton balls were aglow.
I saw a blanket of peace,
Where others had walked through,
... And I remembered our day;
... Gloved hands ... red noses.
As I slept, ... every thought was of you.

There is nothing so fresh as crispness after dawn,
When blue shadows ripple across the laden lawn.
Foxes' prints where they scavenged the whole of night,
In search of food, in the wakening of first light.
A star-like chink of bright breaks behind cold trees,
The longest cast shadows sprawl into fields.
Colour of yellow sees the day's hope glimmer,
Iced leaves glisten in the cold morning winter.
Icicles hanging due south from the tops of homes,
Drip like ice cream from the tips of children's cones.
The distant sky's pastels rise into bolder blues,
Underlined by a straight of mist, in the field's hue.

Observe the shear break of day as December bites.
See triangular geese honker, through their pointed flight.

Troika, troika, troika,
Trotting with high knees,
Jingle, jingle, jingle,
Over land of peace.
Snow so high,
Hooves sink low,
Nostrils blow in the freeze.
... Can you hear winter ?
It's in the horses' wheeze.

... Then came dawn,
... Past my dreams.
... And I awoke.
In the winter deep
The cold night froze streams.
It was now Christmas morning.
... Ribboned gifts I gave to you,
... Colder hands ... warmer mugs,
As we drank ... mulled wine made for two.

Wearing unwrapped slippers we looked through frozen glass, as
Christmas love glowed through our smiles.

5. DeHavilland Trees

Walking the blossom-edged winding path home ...

Georgian balconies feel the wind,
Watch the sweeping rain over the green.
The beech tree leaves signal its seasons;
Full summer foliage to autumn browns.
Then soft snow on rustic fencing,
See snowmen built by cold gloved children.

But I can't wait for spring, so I can see,
Crocus shoot under DeHavilland trees.

The easterly rising spring morning sunshine
Throws yellow light towards the manor.
Southerly, shadows the limestone curve,
Westerly breaks orange across the lawns.
From woodpeckers' first dawn feeding,
Grey squirrels scurry through the cherry leaves,
We can be in no lovelier place.
Daffodils trump under DeHavilland trees.

...

The mere's past still cradles slate roofs,
With woodlands from hundreds of years.
The old manor could tell us history
When traders' horse and carts passed through.
Workers' cottages lined the old lane,
With local grey flint set within their walls.
They sit in the glade of crowning beeches,
With bluebells under DeHavilland trees.

...

Pink cherry March blossom breaks the view,
Young catkins are a thousand earrings,
Wait for soft springtime breeze to come to
Scatter ... confetti petals over the lawns.
Woodpeckers' hammers ricochet the trees,
Jays incline cross-shaped into woodland.
All this happens within a few weeks,
It's a chapter within our ... DeHavilland trees.

6. The Secret

"Hey, wake up!"
The lovers buttoned coats over their nightshirts.

We tip-toed in hand as dew laid at four,
Bare foot across DeHavilland's daisied lawn.
We headed to the woodland, so dense.
Looked back, as we reached the rustic fence.

One finger to mouth we promise the silence,
A loud "Shhh" that everyone, at bedtime, could hear.
Eyes smirking, we both so tittered,
Last star went home from the night sky littered.

We giggle like naughty school children do,
We hasten, with stretched fingers to follow,
Heads low as though we are smuggled,
Through the overhang of the trees for a snuggle.

We kiss against green of the smooth bark tree,
Nature's sensual lovers' spirit born.
The dawning of a moment to share,
Dew on the ground, but lust passed through the air.

Oh how I want you.

I want to devour you.

As I kissed your neck,
I felt the warmth from your breasts.
As I unbuttoned your coat,
My top lip followed your throat.

As I caress your hand,
Our shadowed bodies combine.
Your breath warms my bare chest,
I so wanted you undressed.

Oh, how I want you,
I want to devour you.

Mine and your heavy breaths
Mist into morning air.
In romance of love's fire,
Your head backward in desire.

Then in a moment,
Overwhelming sensation.
True love I whispered.
Dawn light, welcomed the nation.

And as the birds choired alleluia,
The so-impassioned moment final-ed.

Our breaths calmer in woodland scent,

Our little secret of a spring morning spent.

7. Lavender for Love

With fingers clasped, I led you through fragrant fields ...

Hand in hand over the bushes we held,
As French lavenders in fields were trimmed.
You told me you love me, I held your heart to me,
Pink flowers were pinned on your hat's cloth brim.

In joyous step we skipped as we sang,
A bonny tune, of love, that we'd learned.
I gave you my pendant, cherish and hold it,
Love glows on your neckline, where your heart does yearn.

Cherish and hold it.

We circled, arms stretched, point toes to toes,
In meadows, with sun on our backs, so warm.
Blown kisses towards you, you told me forever,
As magnolia blossoms scattered the lawn.

As breeze blew through spring, what seemed as sleet,
Was apple blossom sprinkling Sunday air.
Hands waved through it, church bells were ringing,
We laughed a thought of confetti in your hair.

We danced through bluebells, in the month of May,
The violet waves broke ripples of shade.
Crouching you snap me, my face beams for you,
Shafts of sun found us in woodland-lit glade.

Skywards we kicked legs, with leaves on boots,
Dry acorn cups where bluebells should grow.
Enchanted you kiss me, eyes that adore you,
Sunlight of oak wood, through your hair glowed.

My eyes adored you.

We cycled through tulips, to smell fresh scent,
Windmill sails turned with gentlest breeze.
Red petal ovals turned towards blue skies,
Hands held, lit faces, we kissed on our knees.

We smile across sunflowers, aligned in fields,
Large-petalled flowers all looking south.
You stood so upright, smiled to the sun,
Hands held through stems, my lips met your mouth.

We smelt flowered-rape fields, honied in scent,
Our noses point skywards, inhaling sweet airs.
Oceans of yellow broken by hedges of green,
Sun glowed on our chins, spring wind caught your hair.

Spring wind caught your hair.

In sprinkle rain we stood, pointing at rainbows,
Arches of colour twinned, fronting dark cloud.
I told you we're lucky, together we're gold,
Under streams of sunlight I held you so proud.

Gazing at stars that dotted our worlds,
In gloved hands, together we swooned.
I show you blue Venus, you show me your smile,
Your lips will meet mine, below waning moons.

...

We rode up and down the Christmas carousel,
Circling music, gold horses do pound.
I gave you my left hand ... you gave me your heart,
Dizzy, ... in love, we're going around, and around.

...

Clasped in my hand ... so you'll never forget,

French lavender picked ... in satin blue ribbon.

Pressed to your heart ... a fragrance so sweet,

Stringed by a label ... with love ... they are given.

8. DeHavilland Easter

After green woodpeckers, at first light, chattered away,
As beech leaves turned bright green within a few days,
As warmer days beat frost nights, so were here to stay,
The children that hibernated, to the grass, came to play.

Goodbye crocus, tulips, daffodils, we are now nearly May,
Easter has gone, when DeHavilland respected and prayed.
As kites glided, looking for food, in a windy aerial display,
Foxes called their family, under woodland, at break of day.

French doors on balconies, lie open to take sunshine days,
Red woodpeckers hammered trees, nesting holes, to stay,
Squirrels scampered up cherry bark, with their mates to play,

....

Petals lined the winding path, ... as blossoms were blown away.

9. Lansdowne Crescent

Meet me at dusk at Lansdowne Crescent,
In the shade of the horse chestnut tree,
With towering blooms of spring sweetness,
A glint of sun through its leaves.
Where iron gates are shaped as love hearts,
In walls of Georgian manor gardens,
A kiss for the love I adore,
And a view that you will not believe.

Parade hand in hand along Lansdowne,
The sun will set o'er Worcester city,
Where steeples and towers cut the skyline,
And Victorian roofs are many.
Where holding hands combines two hearts,
The wall as a seat for the colour display.
Hand held with my sunset love,
When silence and thoughts cost a penny.

I met my love in front of Edgar Tower
As the cathedral peeled its bells.
A crown-vaulted gateway behind old doors,
The warmest of hugs was heaven.
Rambling roses across Georgian frames,
As we walk in-hand over College Yard green.
Kisses for my springtime love,
As we stand at the wall to The Severn.

And the world didn't matter.

Skipping heart to heart along The Severn,
We circle and dance, hands holding hands,
Passed lopped trees and centuried cottages,
We laughed and smiled to love.
White swans with signets swam two by two,
The arches on the bridge were lit like jewels,
A big smile for my evening girl,
As the moon shone over us from above.

Hearing dawn-side bells I kiss my love,
Good Friday by the lock on the bridge.
Darkened water coloured by rising morn,
We embrace in button coats.
In chill of shade we hold glove to glove,
Coffee and hugs are refreshing our souls.
Warmed lips for my canal-side love,
Gold painted names on flowerpot boats.

The flowerpot boats became our neighbours,
Picnic blanket to the canal-side bank.
With afternoon sun patterned through the trees,
We sat, legs stretched, shoes on grass.
Fizz popped, we salute flute to flute,
Bubbles and smiles cheer sun-drenched eyes,
Prosecco lips for my blanket love,
Un roman d'amour, read 'loud, makes time pass.

...

As the clock struck ten, I met my true love
With a beaming smile at the Guild Hall gates.
With golden tips, approved by The Queen,
I kissed your fresh rouged lips.
In light rain we talked mind to mind,
An umbrella for two with drips off the brim.
Rubbing noses with my cover love,
We cosied and walked, fingers on hips.

And the rain didn't matter.
On dark blue canvas it splattered ...

Sunlight broke behind cloud.
We smiled together, so proud ...

Sun's reflection on the paving sheen,
... Shoeprints moment, where we had been.

– – – –

As spring became summer,
Days became warmer,
Trousers were now shorts,
Jumpers became shirts.

You wore the prettiest blouse,
Ruffled white open collar,
A smile for the weekend,
With pleated polka-dot skirt.

– – – –

10. Piano Man

The piano man plays introduction,
A pirouette of notes to approach the floor,
Man takes his date with desired firmness.
A single spin on her right foot,
To recoil under his arm.
Nerves will soon become passion,
The look, the smile, the eyes will adore.

There's a note for each church stone laid,
That leads the crowd's eyes to a seated man,
He plays for the Gods below high arches.
Oak pews are queueing in lines,
Statues stand in subdued light,
Piano man is composing.
We are subjects in the artist's plan.

Passion through piano man's fingers
Become a sentiment in our mind's own song,
Colours change with the notes rolling scales.

The musical pause holds thought.

The flat note softens all glory.

A light melody follows through,

The piano man is leading us on.

With recurring love he plays to the crowd,
From the tiniest tinkling, to the drumming resound,
I've become a ballet dancer in my mind.
The lightest of toes as I glide,
Her stretched fingers to meet mine.
With arched back, she swoons.
Lights catch lovers' hearts that pound.

...

He's not there for the glory of God,
Yet he fills the vaults with treasures.
Standing still, I'm captured by his music.
As The Wedding is being played,

Each note is the gentle of lovers,

Each pause is the patience that waits,
Giving two hearts, forsaking all others.

Through to the final note
Their lifetime vows are given.
As the piper plays, the wind blows,
On the sands, waves have riven.

By the loch he leads his new wife
To the shore, on the pebbled beach,

Hands held with a glisten of tears,
... Real life is a world away.

Let these two betrothed lovers,
Forever, be this way.

...

With spotlight on the played open grand,
My fingers are sliding along its shining curve,
Gliding slowly over polished black ebony.

The turned legs reflect the light.

Polished shoes meet golden pedals.

Ten fingers strike the final chord ...

Head bows, as though he came to serve.

11. Dreaming

There's a thought in your head as you smile to white,
Caressing your glass to your loosened shirt,
You are beside a blazing log fire,
Bare feet curled under, your bright eyes flirt.

Georgian frames angle sun across the cills,
Whilst you sleep, I wonder of your dreams.
Your world is in white cotton pillows,
Your hands curve to crumple their seams.

I caress you, hands stroke, sunlit in yellow.
Cuddle into me, your head on my chest.
My fingers slipping into gaping buttons,
Blue and white stripes curve to your breast.

Come to me, adore me, feel me and just touch me,
Let your mind go to a fantastical land.
We will make weekend love in morning light,
Then rest your head and hold hand into hand.

...

Our eyes glint with adoration.
Our smiles are tell-tale signs.
And we laugh a childish laugh
That sniggers, like our younger years.
And if our hearts melt, now and then,
It might be our minds saying "I love you".

Cheeks glow consideration.
Bashfulness is a lover's enchant,
But it will be blue eyes that look to adore you,
They've been there since our very start.

Come to me, adore me, feel me and touch me.

We walk through DeHavilland autumn leaves.
Squirrels foraging to make their winter store,
Woodpeckers are heard through russet trees.

The deer wander across the parkland in dusk light.
Sun now colder, lows much earlier to bed,
The owl hoots through the windswept dark night,

The foxes skulk with October coats bright.

Through my life's angst, heartache, loss and tears,
I will never forget my DeHavilland years.

12. The Childhood Beach

Shhh ... he said.

The hush of air passed through that shell,
It blew seaside dreams to my ears,
Long days playing on watery shores,
I heard the childhood of my yesteryears.

Tshhh ... said the waves.

I saw myself standing to the waves,
But looking back up the beach to see,
My parents laughing whilst they talked,
Smiling, they waved and watched over me.

The children shrilled.

The waves crashed to a white foam fizz,
Wet points left behind as they lowed.
My toes gripping into the sand,
Were ever-sinking as the tide flowed.

The kiddies laughed.

In slow motion I had imagined,
Hot summers and childhood days long.
Children squealed, parents paddled,
The seaside noises were in full song.

Grey seagulls circled.

"Come back Neil, don't go out too far",
My mother's voice called over beach fun.
Light shimmered in heat across my view,
My eyes crumpled in the sharpest sun.

A silent wave ...

I waved back with grabbing child fingers,

My eyes, watery, squinted in the sun.

So childlike, I was, with the biggest smile.

The same hearing shell in my hand.

I took his shell from my ear, and so realised,

Memories of Mum, and Dad ... since he died.

13. The History of Man

Remember, remember, the fifth of November ...

Have you ever touched the history of a building?
The coldness of marble, warmth of terracotta.
You can imagine ancient times under your palm.
Historical men of hard labour, whoever built it,
Through long hours, through days, through months.

Brushing my finger, did I feel history in his cheek?
The warmth of his pale skin, his hand soon to be quite cold.
And I imagined the pain that he bore to this day,
Our history together and how our bond was built.
Sunny days, sunshine months, sunshine years.

...

My mind reheard the early morning phone ring and ring.
Frightened hesitation, followed rude awakening.
I had thought the worst as I looked at the clock.
There could never be good news from a call so early.
Hands ticking, seconds ticking, ... ticking, ... ticking.

...

Sat beside him, I saw worry furrows that were lines,
Disappear from his head, become a smoother brow.

As I spoke, I imagined he could hear my last goodbye.

This part of history now complete, lest forgotten.
My sad memory, for sorrow years, ... for my life.

That hand held remains a thought *forever* held.

— — — —

And as I kissed his forehead,
And looked into his eyes,
I realised, how my gesture of love
Was insignificant, ... to the lifetime he had given ... to me.

— — — —

14. 78 Years

And then darkness fell.
The last day finalled 78 years of life.

I need to sleep, but I cannot sleep,
I should try to smile, but I cannot smile,
I should be content for the good times
We had together, but I grieve this day,
The pain inside me, never taken away.

And all love was lost.
He said no goodbyes after years of love.

I need my strong dad, so I have no strength,
I should try to live, but I have no life.
To speak his eulogy, is all I can do
With the honesty, love and true respect,
That my dad deserves, he'd never expect.

And only time will tell.
He lies silently over years to come.

I need to be there, so then I can talk,
I tell of my day, and know he listens.

And I am content, that I know he's there.

As a child I would always run to him.
As a man, I can ever confide in him.

15. Let's Go With The Rain

Let's go with the rain,
As we don't know what tomorrow may bring.
Today, our hearts might have fallen,
Let us look back at what we were,
How a memory seems a forever thought,
But there will be sunshine, in our lives again.

Let's go with the snow.
It's only been weeks since we lost our love.
Today, our worlds are consumed,
An early winter has set in.
We cannot focus on today or the future,
In grief, we haven't any direction to go.

And as for the sunshine,
That is for others, to brighten their days.
Today, our minds grieve loss,
But now winter has turned to spring,
Blossom is filling our hearts and minds,
Together, we're feeling the healing of time.

And now, everything I need to share with you,
I have to come and be there with you.

16. The Box

I'm wrapping a little box.
There is nothing in it.

A blue box with a lid.
With nothing placed to it.

I'm wrapping a little box,
With silver paper.
Folded with tape edges.
There is nothing in it.

My fingers gently fold the corners,
My mind greatly holds the thoughts.

My scissors cut the sticking tape,
My love can't cut feelings so great.

I'm sat, legs to side,
Upon the rug,
Wrapping a little box,
With frost-colour paper,
Squared sharp, the edges.

Silken is Christmas ribbon,
That crosses the gift, given.

There's nothing placed in it.

I'm sat in the candlelight,
By the fireside,
The glow to warm my face.
My eyes, my half smile, my passion,
Says almost everything.

Red is the stringed label
To my blue box.
Wrapped in silver paper.
Sharp square are the corners,
With taped folded ends,
Written to the other side,
It reads –

'To me, Lots of Love Dad'
With kisses many,
The letter curls tell pride.

My box is placed under the tree,
Beside the many larger presents.
They all have a gift within each.

But my self-wrapped box isn't empty,
... It is full of memories.

It is wrapped with love,
As you gave to me.

The triangle ends hug the box,
As you did to me.

The bow is a beautiful heart,
Your's given for free.

But the words are just simple;
No explanation.
No exclamation.
That mean everything to see.

Memories of Christmases last,
When we were still a family,
When your presence warmed the house,
When your smile warmed our hearts.

My box is closed, papered, folded,
Taped, bowed and placed under the tree.

Memories of Christmas mornings,
When my face was a picture of wonder,
When the presents were bigger than me.

Please don't think it
Of me, so selfish,
That I have wrapped a box,
On your behalf,
Just so I remember each Christmas past.

Please don't think it
Be the only gift,
That you ever left for me.
'Cus in my mind,
My character, is my grounding held dear.

December is not the same
Since you have died.

Each festive season I weep
For you, a few realisation tears.

Under the green perennial tree,
That is dressed to glee,
Each bauble is a souvenir,
The tinsel, a hug of a scarf ....

I need the gifted memories' box,
That'll become larger every year.

....

When it comes to New Year's Eve,
All presents have been opened,
There is just one I leave ...

One still bowed under the tree.

It sits as I remember times,
Memories to haunt my fears,
And those where love chimes,

Kissed thoughts for Auld Lang Syne.

....

On New Year's Day I dismantle the tree,
Not just a Christian symbol or Pagan belief,

But a pyramid of love and hope.

Atop is the star to replicate the sky,
That is yours, that's fallen to take its place with pride.

Each bauble is a delicate sphere of love,
That reflects a world of emptiness, with you above.

And heart-shape bows tied across the green,
Are each a year of thought to ever-lasting dreams.

Each, a souvenir to help me cope.

With baubles packed to a box,
Untied bows are not untied connections.
The star will ever shine in my mind.

The tinsel I unwrap from the tree,
To then wind it forever around me ...

A hug of the Christmas tree's scarf,
As I store away my wrapped box of memories.
That I brush close to tickle my side.

My pyramid is the kindred tree ... to which I abide.

17. DeHavilland Tears

As I looked east, across curved wrought iron balconies,
With warm mug cupped between hands,
Orange sun was hung in morning tide sky.

A tear for Dad rolled down my cheek.

The artist had swept the sky with more light.

As if he brought hope out of darkness,
The day said goodbye, to the memory of night.

Walking down the well-trodden woodland path,
The last of damp, had left fresh spring air.
Bluebells scented the sidelines to our view.

I remembered my last day with Dad.

The artist's fine tip, picked out violet strands.

As I palmed the side of my right cheek,
The pain of thoughts, left tears in my hands.

...

And on the first Father's Day, since his death,
The poet sat afoot of his grave.
His gesture of flowers wrapped in ribbon.

And he read aloud his poems of love.

The artist's brush painted silver on dark cloud.

The last of blossom blew through the air.

In my heart he told me, he was so, so proud.

...

As I looked into the early evening,
Through the crowns of twigged beeches,
White sun smudged in grey pastel skies.

Memory of Dad, I held so dear.

The artist had dripped his full brush wash.

As if they empathised my own thought,
So the clouds wept DeHavilland tears.

The clouds wept DeHavilland tears

The best church is not necessarily
The one with the biggest dome or spire,
Or that with the most people.

Stand in nature's church.
Behold your family church.
You, as a self-church (to believe in yourself).

Then decide.

The Love Hundred

The Cathedral Of Chess

You could hear black and white keys playing chorales
Through a cathedral, tinted in sepia light,
To go back in time to the dawning Christians.

The doors of oak latch open to eternity
To walk the righteous path, of The Book's psalms,
Following footsteps of martyrs and saints.

You could almost hear a whisper, through high arches,
Passed the organ flutes, down to the altar,
Where thrones should stand for seated lords.

You could kiss read pillars, that climb to heaven,
Fingers could splay, slow, up each of the curves,
Trying to reach, and touch the clouds of gods.

You could look through the shaft sunlight from windows,
To high stained glass arches, woven with lead,
To glimpse a view, the flight of winged angels.

You can walk the stone pathway of devoted pilgrims,
That have prayed at the tall candlestick altar,
Following the lead, of legended disciples.

Where stained glass shows saints
Beside a blond cherub child,
Where bishops are two dimensional soldiers,
Where the clergy are enshrined,
As though they are second to God,
By raised scripture carvings, they reside.

Where cloisters are webs over
The prey they aim to catch,
Where marble chequered floors are the game of chess
And most of us the playing pawns,
The bishop stands to the king,
The God's army pieces, serve to win match.

And

One thousand mouths, are singing alleluia,
To show their commitment to the meaning of life.
And their redemption? ... to reach the higher heavens.

A hand-figured cross,
A doff of a gent's cap,
A skirted slow curtsy,
A bow of head, ... is their respect.

But I stand, back to the wall.
The cool stone as my stay.
Beyond all the glory,
I'm here, for nothing ... except ...

2. The Angel

And in my moment,
I just stood ... and stared.

...

The window threw sunbeams across the wall,
As though highlighting my thought.

Looking higher than myself,
Looking through gladed dust,
Looking to a vision, of the enshrined trust ...

A eulogy of beautiful sculpture,
Mounted in chiselled lime.

Far from the pompous of the church,
Far from the singing of the choirs,
Far from pillars and pinnacle spires ...

It captured, ... how one man is not alone.

The battle-beaten soldier, wounded, fell.
As an angel held him, ... she had the biggest wings.
And the fallen's onlooking wartime friend
Showed the most pallored face from hell.

He knew, with sabre in scabbard, from his waist,
And bugle draped, as a sling over one shoulder,
His soldier from the field of red poppies,
Was in best hands .... death to his face.

...

Although, in my mind, I have always heard
The organ of acceptance and repentance
Through the church, of God's soldiers,
In that moment, I heard the bugle take slack ...

The bugle to rally the army,
The bugle as horses galloped,
The bugle to help triumph,

As soldiers came under attack.

And on the death of the heroes,
On the death of lamed horses,
On the death, ... of a fallen nation,

The final notes, of The Last Post, came back ...

One comrade with tears in eyes,
One comrade played true salute,
One comrade, a shadow to sun,
One comrade, ... to hold the country as one.

3. The People's Hope

After the bells have played for sheer hours,
Over the city, with overwhelming power,

On woven green cushions, where knees have prayed,
Where thoughts of belief, make a believer's day.

After the trinity doctrine has been taught,
Commanding embreachment of one's own thought,

On hallowed church ground, the holy communion,
To bring the priest's flock, to Christ's own union,

The people's prayer, ... is the people's hope.
As generations fell, it became, ... their way to cope.

4. The Candle

In the silence of the church, with sepia hue ...

I'm lighting a candle to remember you,
A silent commitment, you are not forgotten.
The death of my father, to continual grief,
My single flame gesture, is some relief.

I see the whisp of flame flicker, as though a wink,
The kindred smoke, in the spirit's waved rise,
A belief of the memories that it spells,
From beloved family, to when you fell ...

My love is a hundred of red field poppies,
My heart cries the rains, on which they feed.
As my mind gushes, the more the storms,
The more the memory, the love hundred sprawls.

The nimbus clouds follow the long horizon,
Through skies of red, ... the colour my heart's bled.
They're the kindred train, leading to you,
I couldn't help but stare, with memories true.

In the blossom of spring, the birds mate and sing,
After winter migration, with happy refrain.
It was they that flew, into October skies,
And didn't realise, early winter you died.

...

I tried to snub the wick between my fingers,
Rubbed them to see fingertips of grey soot,
... But, I relit the kindred love candle again,
It brought back a smile, seeing the ever flame.

...

I saw you as my bowed tree, under I stood,
When lightning struck, and life's thunders rolled.
I could stretch my hand out, to feel the last rains,
You let me walk alone, momentum regained.

Every dandelion seed that floats in the air,
Every white feather, that falls slow to the ground,
Maybe God's sign, that you are walking beside me,
Your continual spirit, is our kindred pride.

My lit candle is my own hope.

My words to you, help me cope.

...

I could grab the greying candle smoke,
And hold it in my whiten fist,
To capture every memory.
That clench, would be, forever kissed.

5. Hope and Dreams

The father cradles his new-born son,
Day rising through the window of life.
Arms of comfort, that show love,
Tiny fingers, wrap to Daddy's thumb.

The innocent mind, that cannot think,
The blurred eyes, that cannot quite see,
The open mouth, that speaks hunger,
Is the start of hope, on his first blink.

...

I hold the dream, that you will better me,
That you'll see more, than I ever did see.

I hold the dream, that your health will be best,
Your goodness of heart, will beat in your chest.

I hold the dream, that you'll be a prince,
And meet a princess, to live a life of bliss.

If truth be told, I also, ... hold a dream,
That our family bond ... ever reigns supreme.

...

I want you to roll through The Chilterns,
Jubilant poppies peek their heads through grain,

And run through springtime beech woodlands,
Bluebells lay silent, as their Sunday display.

Beech trees are pillars, to reach to the skies,
Their canopy makes nature's temple of play.

Look from them, through leafed arch windows,
See father and son walk through the fields of May.

...

We've built our father/son team.
My baby ... holds his hopes,
My loving ... holds our dreams.

...

My hundred has a new-growth sapling tree,
Well nurtured, he'll grow much taller than me.

6. The Father's Hug

As a child I would sit by you, hand on knee,
As you walked through the door, run to hug your legs.
Your one hand on my back to reassure,
I'd know your cologne ... and the smell of your breath.

Why did you not hug me, as a man to a man ?
It would be the deepest feeling, beating all others.
Security bound a father to son,
Was it so wrong to hold your man child's arms ?

Can my selfishness be condemned ?
Does reversion to innocence make amends ?
For all I now want, covers my regret,
Greatly over-thought, are my dreams spent.

I want to be the cottage bayed window,
Your rambling rose, as a hug over my shoulder,
With open flowers that spell me love,
Your petalled-kiss to comfort my brow.

Your squared man hands would curve to hold me,
To soften your heart, and pretence of physical touch.
Your commitment to be forever,
My never forgotten, throughout my life.

...

As I saw you lying so calmly, suited in state,
I told you that I'd be alright, after you're gone.
You must have known what I would become,
... You could have told me, but didn't reply.

...

I realised I was the blond cherub child,
And you were the saint, standing by.

You could have told me, but you didn't reply.

7.

My hundred blooms all year long,
No matter how I try,
The poppies keep on sprawling,
And will not ever die.

And the dandelions stand between,
Seed heads are held high.
Every month is forever spring,
A thousand fairies, ... will ever fly.

8. Church of Beeches

I took my son to the church of beeches,
That climb higher than our eyes reach.
We took the kindred candle of love,
And thought of you as far above.

Your grandfather would prefer you to play,
Than stand in pews, and so pray.
As he was always a man of fresh air,
We've brought his candle, so he can share.

We've brought his candle, so he can share.

And the branches joined as cloisters arched,

And light shafted through leaves of March.

And beech pillars, to skies reached.

We sat in silence, without church's preach.

We sat in silence.

We looked out through arched window beeches,
Across my hundred of rolling light,
And in the content of our own hearts,
There wasn't a single poppy in sight.

Not a single red poppy.

And I hugged my son, through heart of my love,
I saw your candle burn more than bright.
Your wink of flame, told me how you feel.
To feel your son's soul, shows a man's might.

To feel your son's soul, *shows* a man's might.

...

And to his forehead, my petalled lips,
That said a lot more ... than a father's grip.

...

And blowing through the high branches,
Was your voice, heard in nature's whisp.

9. The Nightmare

I dreamed that night of my hundred of red poppies,
That came back, after emotions flowed ...

I saw you walking towards me,
Through ten thousand red flowers.

You walked as the handsome man,
The man, with a beautiful smile.
The man with a crisp white shirt,
The man, whose eyes brightly flirt.

I could almost smell childhood cologne,
I smelt the memory of your breath.
I was sat upon your shoulders.
I swung on your arms stretched.

...

And before my words could tell,

My heart died ...

As, to ground ... suddenly, you fell.

And my pallored face was sheer white,
As, through illness, you fell to life's plight.

I looked up to the bluest skies,
Expectant the angel of wings would fly by.

...

My night cries recalled the cathedral.
My moment when I stared.
Where was my angel of mercy
To give gracious love, only she could share ?

...

I have to think of your illness pathway,
As though we were a family at battle,
As though enemy was constant attack,
As though, ... we were rallying beside you.

Even then, I held the kindred lantern,
The lantern where the flame was bright.
The lantern that held your spirits true,
The lantern, ... to lead our family through.

10. The Family Window

In my mind's sepia hue church,
You are my pillars of strength.
The altar holds the tallest candle.
The cloisters bow over, to hold me.

The chequered floor beneath my feet,
I realise, is life's game of chess,
Where there is not a single pathway,
And is played without bishop or queen.

....

Our woven glass family window
Stands higher than any church's.
Stands more for life and its meaning,
Stands as picture to our hearts' bleeding.

Our framed glass family album
Shows an ever light shines through.
Shows we all sat on your shoulder,
Shows no two dimensional soldiers.

And ....
Our minds' arched window is open
Until every psalm has been read,
Until our lives are fully defined,
Until, next to your love ... we are enshrined.

And finally, after I've ever kept looking,
... A glimpse of the winged angel flies behind.

11. The Bugle

And as *The Last Post* is played
On the 5th of November,
Resonating through the winter's air,
Is the bugle's final note.

The bugle's quivering last note.

The bugle's ever-strong last note.

Fallen leaves that lay at my feet,
Empathise my fallen heart.

I cry again, in winter rain,
As words get stuck in my throat.

...

And my sapling is now his own man.
To pay his own pilgrimage, to
His grandfather's life's steps,

To his own hundred, he should stand.

12. The Hundred of Memories

My hundred of love poppies,
Is now millions of flowers,
They all stand with new buds
Saluting to petal heads of red.

And,
One billion fairies float your love,
They're swathing the hundred's air,
A trillion memories over fields,
As dandelions blow 'way their heads.

The birds stayed this first winter,
They circle the hundred in display,
Singing low, a less colourful tune,
They are here, ... to pay their respects.

And the clouds' cheeks are of grey,
Sky of colour, is another day.
Hanging heads, shoulder to shoulder,
They are bowing, to, ... acknowledge the dead.

...

And I hold my hand to heart.

And I stand in my silence.

And I cry the hardest tears,

As a sign of, not just respect,
... Nor the love you'd expect,

... But a sign, ... of all I regret.

My hundred is a million poppies ...

Our brothers may fight in arms,
But the real strength is
Their home country holding hands,
Together in solidarity.

To smile when you leave,
Is the memory that stays with me.

The War Years Pentalogy

Twenty Hundred to Southampton

Slow, every minute of the clock, ticked.

As the steam train's bags were load,
Backward plumes to billow fog built,
Haunting, each and every chimney blow.
Heartbeat rhythm, wheels across tracks,
Would meet each, torched-lit rails' gaps,
When it pulled away slow.

Hoarse was the steam train's blow.

As light from station lantern glowed,
Nervous flame licked to evening wind,
That stretched to a cobbled shadow,
That reflected glimmer as walls napped.
Bricks highlight over arches, lapped,
We stood in the half-light thrown.

Deep were the steam train's woes.

Step into carriages, doors closed,
The latches clicked, handles turned,
The slide of glass, brass windows lowed.
Uniformed men for country and king,
Their regiment boots shined to sheen,
Catching the train to wartime zones.

Leaving children to their homes.

The first whistle blew, we rub nose to nose,
Timetable letters flicked in turn,
Their fast tapping, as though sending in code.
One last kiss to keep your dreams,
This my promise, to know what might be.
The final call from mute megaphone.

I'm just another soldier
To the wartime zone.

The station clock tocked the last second slow,
Master's whistle shrilled to a kick,
Southampton twenty hundred hours must go.
Platform wives hold their great esteem,
A kiss to air is love, luck and go free,

Yet inside each, their anxious heart froze.

To wave fast hands
To faster train blows.

Tear handkerchiefs to every eye goes,
Open windows, lovers hand-kissed,
Waving back, as their steamed hair was blown.
Assurance smiles to keep all dreams,
As luck of fate, to those men is deemed.
They'll fight to fields, where poppies do grow.

The load is brave men,
Baggage .... and lives as stow.

Steam flowed Victorian arches below.
White plumes fog the garrison town,
As though a blanket to the factories thrown.
The vwoof broke the darkened serene,
Lanterns lit side-lined misted trees,
As the black painted locomotive lowed.

Off to the coast, the
Coal-laden engine tows.

Left to the station, silhouettes in mist.

Women, children, as return brakes hissed.

Statued figures are many, but so alone.

None to know if their men would come home.

The hanging clock took forever to click.

Sick to their core, the contagion of war.

Onward to the battle zone ...
Four hundred did go,
Four hundred did go,
Four hundred did go,

On the hoarse train of woes.

Listen, the beating heart, quieter
To the distant night, lamp-lit, she hacks.

The hazed torch to where she goes.
Farewell all, her forlorn whistle blows.

...

Head in hands, the seated men distraught.
Those standing stared each other's eyes,
No expression, shoulders crammed doors.

Not a single mouth moved.

There was fright to their whites.

Nobody spoke what they were going for.

...

Listen ... the heartbeat on tracks.
It might be the only one return back.

Four hundred did go,
Four hundred did go,
Four hundred did go ...

Ribbon Tail Kite

1.

Stand to envy the dreams of
The young child's wonder mind.

With arms fully-stretched high,
Tip-toed in sandaled shoe,
His fingers flared to a wide,
As he let his balloon to fly.

One of many with their labels,
Written with their name and hearts,
Fifty little pairs of hands,
Whispered all fond goodbyes.

Each balloon to higher than high,
Wonderment stilled ... as they touched the sky.

Each held the child's dreams,
Where would the red balloon go to?
Beyond the hedge?
Beyond the village?
To the seaside coast?
An unknown place?
To think of many, they will try.

"Goodbye balloon, goodbye."

Each red heart to higher than high,
The biplane's cross passes the child's arms by.

2.

And the child that builds his dreams in sand,
Has the admiration of the older man.

He can dig, bare foot, his hole,
In hope to get to the earth's core.
Only dug two spades down,
It seems the deepest hole of all.

He may bury himself inside,
And fill sand to his neck above.
Then laugh until he cries,
His head to the beach, as a ball.

That child will ever dream of his feat,
But not know the meaning that lies beneath.

And he will build his own castle,
With flag to the seashore wind.
This, his dream to build an empire,
As a biplane flies over the turreted mounds …

With engine noise so loud, the children's laughter is so drowned.

To sky is the sight of kites,
That shimmer to gazing sun.
Wonderment to control freedom,
As they dip and swirl in their flight.

He points above his height.

Be in awe of the ribbon tail kite,
It is freedom above the innocent crowds.

3.

The older child climbs the great leafed oak,
For a better view above the free man's land.

He climbs the trunk to the split,
He climbs branch to another,
He climbs to the leafed bow end,
And stands on the grand tree's yoke.

Intent to get closer to the sky,
The best of views is his goal,
To say that he climbed the mighty tree.
Beyond his field, streaming is grey smoke.

Closer to the white tail kites.

Floating diamonds.

Sunlit as jewels,

That fly, … early morning sunrise skies.

Higher to see planes flying by,
Far between many kites' strings,
That glisten in the low sunlight,
Angled as though tethered guys.

Beware how often the biplane passes by,
His mum and dad said they might be spies.

On far horizon, the largest white balloon,
Strung in the morning tide dews.
Wonderment how big it really could be,
It holds men for many hours, high to sky.

The white balloon is held to its tie,
Hanging in yellow hue morning's rise shine.

4.

The women stand behind window frames,
White net curtains hiding their eyes.
Binoculars peering beyond
The children, ... that fly, morning light kites.

All men were called to fight for country and king,
They dug their own trenches to the ground,
In boot, to defend their own castle,
Hiding behind the earthen mounds ...

The rumble of biplanes flying low in sound,
The peacetime's skies were ever drowned.

...

Still standing was the shade of the oak tree,
Where children hid from planes that pry.
Praying their fathers to come home,
Bombs are falling to the distant ground.

Mothers were calling in their playing child,
Kites held in arm, their freedom denied.

...

The little hands held to the window,
His nose pressed to glass dripped with dew,
His eyes fix to the big silver balloon,

The oak field turned grey,
Became night during day,

The haunt of war shaded the sky.

A Zeppelin attacking the country's pride.

...

He wondered of his red balloon,
Sent as wishes to his father,
Stringed love and four kisses,

Not knowing he had already died.

When told the balloon never arrived,
With bewilder eyes the boy cried and cried.

"Goodbye Papa, goodbye."

...

Nothing could ever replace his father,

The image masked his sky balloon,

The kites' diamonds, above spring dew.

Beautiful yellow sky.

Their tails squiggled,

Against wisp cloud on high.

The noise of the distant planes that flew.

The teardrop-shape, observation crew.

The Zeppelin hung over his long goodbye.

The images scarred to his mind's eye.

5.

The scars of the years forever brew,
And remain there, ever instilled.

Never question the lack of will,
Of the elderly lady;
With her bottom to a bench,

With her walking stick central,
Leant, with two hands
Covering its arch handle.

For every crag to her face,
Her eyes, now dulled with age,
Lips thin, that hold firm her tale.

For she has seen man of wars,
The beauty of child being born,
The death of her life-long husband.

For she laughed with best friends,
Loved, cared for close company,
... Then held their hands, to dying end.

Her mind remembers halcyon days,
She walked in hand as a young lady,
Sun beating down on the lovers,
As their hands swathed the feather corn.

Where love was a bite through a red strawberry,
Sunshine caught her eyes to half-closed.
Picnic blanket for two by water,
Boats sailed passed with war-end bunting.

Never question her lack of will,
Until you have felt ...

What she can feel.

6.

When war peace is long time dealt,
The mind still chews a bitter pill.

Never think indifferent or ill,
Of the older gentleman,
Sat beneath the same oak tree.
Eyes straight forward and then
They view side to side,
With knowledge more than younger men.

For every tear coming to eye,
Is a memory to his mind,
That still haunts his every day.

For he was the man to the war,
Just twenty years, when he flew,
… Naive to how he was to serve.

Under this great tree he has watched seasons;
Year on year, springtime flowers flourished,
The oak shaded him through hot summer,
Autumn's felled leaves, winter's snow.

In fields far beyond he fought the enemy,
Rifle to hand, ammunition to belt,
His last goodbyes with dirt to face,
Watching his fellow comrades razed to death.

Never question his tear to eye,
Until you listen,
… The words to his breath.

You'll never see what's in his sight.

Once, he also ran the grass field,
A ball of string to his hand.

Freedom of the ribbon tail flight,
Freedom he fought for, … with all might.

7.

Just stand in awe of windswept freedom.
Every red diamond, white ribbon-tailed kite –

Patriotic, against a backdrop blue sky.

The Homecoming

Victorian arches held up the tracks,
Trains going from places to places.
Rhythmic wheels heard across the gaps,
To another town ... then they'd be back.

Their movements more often, now end of war,
The soldiers coming home from bases,
Red, white and blue streets, buntings flaunt,
Last weekend, to good years we'd brag.

Anthems of voices, to the flown flag.

Our mums b'n working as factory lags,
Their hair tied back, grease to their faces.
Chimneys still plume to the skies,
Until the time bell, hails last hour.

Kids run cobble streets.
Kicked balls, untied laces.
Prayers as sunsets lie.
Bedsides, as church pews.

We cheered, arms high, "God save the king !"

The union flag to the mast flew,
Reflected glad faces, red, white and blue.

Victorian trackways to tall brick arches,
The locos chuff lateral at great pace,
Percussion steam heads parallel tracks,
... Pull to the station ... to then about tack.

Now replenishing goods to the stores,
All coal to the fire, faster they're racing,
This last week, the end of the wars,
No more Zeppelins, the terror they bring.

Salute, stand tall, to our jubilant flag.

Our mums have been working, wearing sewn rags,
No makeup, sleeping, no airs, no graces.
Supplying the country's basic need,
The steam horn blows, at the tenth hour.

Kids run terrace rows.
Laundry hung to back yards.
Little food, shelved to stores.
One dinner, now serves two.

With innocent joys, did we all sing!

Proud to be on Britannia's crew,
Proud to be red, white and honourably true.

...

Stand again to the railway platform.
Salute, the train coming to view.

Here she comes.

Slow, she pulled through the rain,
Her steam as a cloud of gloom.

Here she comes.

The short whistle lost its stream,
The arrival of eleven a.m. troops.

Wives and children to wave hello,
Their men returning to their homes.

Here she comes.

There was little heartbeat to the track.
This the last post, to never turn back.

Brakes squealed, last steam hissed,
Women yearn for their kisses missed.

Whistle blew, 'hind anticipation.
Welcome four hundred to the station.

She's here.

...

Handles turned, clack of latches,
Doors opened to home dispatches.

Huf.

Below the bunting; red, white and blue,
To the platform, ... their men but a few.

Three fifty died whilst on tour.
Less than fifty walked the train door.

Huf.

Many helped by comrade shoulders,
The black and blue truth of brave soldiers.

Through silence was heard a dropped pin tack ...

The men walked through steam.
Blurred faces, unseen.

... The women's fears were not held back.

Children's tears welled sacked eyes.
It was years since dads said goodbye.

Huf.

Mothers, wide-eyed, still mouths open.
Clenched their hands with sheer emotion.

...

Exhausted, the hoarse train of woes,
To never tell of what she had known.

...

Then a low note from the ornate clock ...

For every kiss,
Seven were missed.

Toc.

For every hug,
Seven graves dug.

Toc.

For each of relief,
Seven showed grief.

Toc.

Seven to one child,
No father, drawer filed.

...

The men;
Shamed cheeks of red,
With sheer faces of white,
Their depressed minds blue,

How could the bunting hang so true ?

...

The bloody war to be a four year banquet,
The oppressor yearned feasts of meats,
Home-grown from furrowed trenches,
Troops' heads as apple-mouth boars.

Victory would have made great the successor,
So, he called for final helpings;
Simmering hot, the gravy and dumplings ...

Silver dome lifted to a cripples' slaw.

...

They heard no heartbeat to track,
Of the four carriages, only two banked.

With their wives' kisses, ... face-smothered,
Each comrade looked back, ... tears to eyes.

They saw images of fallen remembered,
Thoughts down the track. Reheard their last cries.

They left their friends, true brothers in arms.
No souvenir, were the memories, home-packed.

The hanging clock, its head low.
Each minute ... a condolence bore.

Disbelief blew, the bunting, through.
No celebration, ... for those but few.

The tally list across the ranks.

Four hundred did go,
Four hundred did go,
Four hundred did go.

There is no victory to war.
There is only uncertainty to the
Consequence of circumstance.

Rose De Paris

1.

Through front door of panelled oak,
Let himself in from walking autumn leaf,
With long-shaft key turned in lock,
Into the hallway of stoned tiles.

Long dark coat of finest tweed wool,
Hat of rabbit skin to warm greyed head,
Scarf of stripes in high school colour,
Was wear of his traditional style.

To the bureau, removed gloves,
Black leather, laid straight of finger,
Angled to one forward corner,
By yesterday's post, laid in file.

October autumn brought leaves off trees,
Weekend's wind made patterned pavements,
Gathered deadfall lined the roadside gutters,
Late afternoon sun shone through reddened acer.

The light towards winter lessened,
Damp of rain sheened the walkway,
The table lamp turned to subdue hue,
Boots paralleled to doormat's pile.

2.

This, his favourite time of year,
This, held fond memories past,
Especially of his younger years,
Since a widower ten months last.

He and his wife, Bright Young Things,
They met London in late 1920s,
Teens through grey days of World War 1,
With her pretty face, love grew so fast.

A tea house in Piccadilly,
She sat with friends, bone china to hand,
Casual, with greatest smile, flirted,
With makeup as the 'new woman class'.

She was a flapper, denoted by her dress,
It was summer, warmer, the city heat,
The hem was shorter, tasselled to her open breast,
She wore a bell straw hat to her head.

With elbowed right hand higher,
Gitane smoked, fine line to ceiling,
Her red lips cosied the holder,
Her long gloves, black leather, matched.

3.

And he was a gentleman so dapper,
Worked as a journalist, London east,
Reported on life post-wartime,
Wrote for the young, as fashion police.

They danced the alive of Paris,
With his work, autumn 1929,

Where young lives lived pazazz....

The band played to the rear
Of Les Maisons Du Thé.
Couples danced upbeat jazz.

The ladies shimmied, tassels to their dress,
Gents with slacks, shirt opened to chest.
Cocktails sipped, a new found freedom,
Decade past the war's peacetime pledge.

Gents imitate Valentino,
Ladies copied gloss fashion press.
A vibe to live life as no tomorrow,
After war left young loves depressed.

Girls were now showing their knees,
Rejuvenated, only wanted best.
Chanel coutured flaunten vision,
In bars, they all dressed to impress.

Feather boas, long-stringed pearls,

Deco patterns to their dress,...

The Bright Young Things of Paris town,
Oozed their cocktail society zest.

...

4.

The rambling rose climbs the porchway,
Curled iron, cantilevers the roof,
The large pink blooms long forgotten,
Dried thorny stems curled to the bell.

Over the wet gated pathway,
As confetti in the morning dew,
Summer petals had fell to floor,
No more they fragranced the cottage door.

...

5.

The guys were drinking, happy to be clappers,
Ladies' gold shoes, ever-fast toe tappers.
Dancing outside the streets' salon bars,
Paris really gave it razzamatazz.
Ladies with sequins to their dresses,
The young used all life, they still had.

The cool cats with their chrome grille cars,
Smoking Gitanes hanging from their lips,
Hanging out of windows, whistling at
The belles parading, hands to hips.

The Charleston danced in lines to floor,
Kicking stockings with fancy heels,
Gents two tones kicked low to their side,
The twenties allowed 'do as you feel'.

Ladies all wanted to be Marlene,

Images from Picture Goer magazine.

Gents to be Ramon Navarro,

Greased their hair, to oiled sheen.

The jazz trumpets played a faster beat,
Lindy hop pranced along every street,
Ladies wore trousers, as though men,

(Now new to the capital's scene,)
Not every girl was to be a boa queen.

....

6.

The deaden wisteria hangs twisted,
Over the stone cottage bay window.
This year's growth has now fallen.
Autumn leaves clung to its branches.

Its bow strangled the last light,
Its blossom was long forlorn,
Its fingers bent to the frame,
It was the same plant, only by name.

...

7.

The crowds were dance floor hopping,
Couples were showtime topping,
American-style, lindy dance bopping,
The Paris set, weren't known for stopping.

Jazz at lunchtime, dancing to evening,
Ladies' fashion ever-more revealing,
Bars with over-celebration feeling,
You'd never guess, war minds were reeling.

(Ladies, from men, were fashion stealing.)

Trend magazines glossed the tables,
Decored by poses of Betty Grable,
Images from watercoloured sable,
Watch them parade their fashion labels.

Every weekday were high tea dances,
Beautiful ladies, the apple of glances,
With spat-wearing gents taking chances,
Ladies accepting photograph advances.

Dancers,
Glancers,
Chancers,
Romancers.

The young were playing in their masses.

With short bob cut and swinging fake pearls,
Drop-back dresses, dropped hip line girls,
Coiffured hair with trim glossy curls,
Spinning fast, as high hem lines whirled.

Spenders,
Trenders,
Pretenders,
And
Alter-genders.

Bright Young Things, the post war splendours.

Gents cruised with their big arched wheels,
Ladies made sure their bodies revealed,
This the decade of 'do as you feel',
The best of life was there, as a steal.

...

Like there'd be no more tomorrows,
La romance was the life of the free.

Liberté, Paris,
Liberté.

8.

The young disowned by their mamas and papas,
They saw Bright Young Things as mis-happers,

Generations had fought in the trenches,
Now sequins and spats sang to the benches.

Non-conforming, they were non-life mappers,
Left the oldies at home, as evening nappers.

They danced in jet streams of the war planes.
Their lives saved, lived a life of insane.

Cocktails and mocktails,
They filled the sparkling train.

To every floor the base drum and cymbal,
To gents' slacks with finer black braces,
Ladies' faces, beauty spots and dimples,
The church of dance had the people playing.

....

From the drums of war,
That were still thought raw,

From the sounds of knell,
To the liberty bells.

The enemy, by allies, thwart,
Paris partied, full wind to her sails.

9.

Her boa used as une rose de grâce,
Untied from her neck as a chain.

Son béret bleu thrown towards Eiffel,
Her string of pearls held to her breath.

They romanced as Notre Dame struck ten,
Gants longs off derrière Maison du Thé,

Charlestoned Les Champs E'lysees,
They lindy hopped along La Seine,
Were seen jiving sous L' Arch De Triomphe ...

All this, through dark of the night,
To watch Paris at the break of dawn's day.

...

They sang beneath the liberty bells,
They swung under the lamplight spell,
Held hands, passed ladies, with love to sell,
Spun in circles as autumn leaves fell.
They smooched with chandeliers above,
Passioned within the moon's hue of love,
Caressed noises, heard thrash of doves ...

Her boa blew away as they chased,
Her net stockings removed in haste,
His eyes to a black garter, faced,
Their gin to lips was the French kiss taste.

... And
Between teeth, she held the leathern glove.

...

At six he kissed his English Rose,

By the river's waters of Paris.

Dawn light sur la ville de l'amour,

His proposal to her, they were to marry.

....

10.

In the cottage hallway,
Was his memory of Paris past ...

A mock feather boa they bought
Two years, before she died, ago.

Long gloves she wore autumn last,
As the winds through the village did blow.

A felt coche of acer autumn red,
Until last winter she wore to her head.

These, their memories, did ever last.

....

Through reflective eyes, there is sorrow.

1929.

They lived,
They danced, ... as there was no tomorrow.

But,
Through another World War,
Through children, that she bore,
To watching man land to the moon.

His darling Rose de Paris,
Was not so long ago ...

Another fifty years plus, ... they did borrow.

Love Letters

1.

Do you remember ?

We held hands at the end of Brighton pier?
We were summer loves for '37.
You promised me always,
I promised you ever,
We promised we'd always be together?

We walked in hand along the breaking shore,
No money to pocket, no shoes to feet.
I found the perfect a blue pebble,
You found its twin other,
We laughed that they could be stone beach lovers.

In the late-afternoon sun, shadows long,
As the fairground played on the pier end,
Couples walked the promenade,
Children knelt with bucket and spades,
As though no one was on the beach, although a crowd ...

As I so pushed mine into your palm,

You clenched it tight.

It was the perfect size.

My two hands clasped around yours.

The stone was a heart in your clasp's body,
Your hands a heart in my warm hands, cupped.
At that moment, our eyes of proud,
In the crash of the waves so loud ...

"This, my darling, is a blue stone,
'That we will ever be true stone',
It is the 'We'll never be through stone',
Back to the sea, it never be thrown."

She replied,
My darling, I remember '37.
You, always more than one summer a love.
Your kiss was delicious,
Your hug was forever,
Our fingers clasped, would never so sever.

We sat on the promenade through the sunset,
As handsome was your smile, that I so melted.
The taste of vanilla,
Scrumptious was your kiss,
It is the one thing, my mind, will never so miss.

And I also gave you my found pebble.

To its curved round I kissed,

On its smooth face I wrote,

'Love is life-long, together we'll grow.'

My love will ever so run through my wording,
The blue of stone ever reflects my eyes.
They always adore you,
My arms be here for you,
Our love started with, and should be one so big kiss.

2.

She always pulled the letter from the bottom.

Always laid in received date order.

Always cherished the musty odour.

Always, but never so forgotten.

Sent from her so darling,
Posted from the wars.
Written in the lamplight.
Written by his fair hand.
Written with more love he ever so shared.

With a French stamp.
With two date marks.
With *Military Post* to side.
The envelope of cream,
The writing in black ink,
Where letters looped,

Where words stood slanted,
Where every moment showed that he so cared.

In the first words she remembered seeing him dressed in blue,
As smart as any handsome man, blond quiff, greased.

In the first sentence she remembered waving him goodbye,
Kit bag packed, shoes polished to the gate.

In the paragraphs she envisaged his smile,
When the blow from lips across hand was kissed.

Three months after leaving.
Posted from the wars.
Written from the combat.
Protecting the real truth.
His first communication, she, ... he so missed.

Through his words, neat, dotted, crossed and slanted,
Were the memories of '37 ... so enchanted.

3.

In a row of Victorian cottages,
Terraced through streets, east of London Town,
Was her bedroom with bayed window front,
Blanketed was her single bed,
To the small table her heart would so drown.

On the mantle of the tiled fireplace,
Sat a blue memory box painted by father,
With mirror above to brush her coiffed hair,
A candle was lit to the right side,
To left, the one photo of her so lover.

In the box were nine love letters,
One for each season he had left her so alone,
Each with handwritten address to his lady,
Each with a stamp from a foreign land,

Date timed once from a single country,
Twice from travelling through two,
Military Post to one side …

Each written in bunk light, under night's cover.

Lifting all others neatly stacked in time,
She would always slide the bottom one to read,
With loops in the Ss, slant to writing,
The top sliced open by her nail,
The memory of '37 made her heart bleed.

4.

In her hand was his blue stone,
His 'ever be true stone',
His 'never be through stone'.
Fingers clenched, she'd never be alone.

5.

She sent mail more often than she so received,
Her pen across paper, more than she would so read,
Not knowing his whereabouts, made more her need,
Yet knowing he was her lost blue boy to the seas.

With her paper of pink,
Her written pen of black,
Her envelope of white,
Her stamp was of King George,
She enclosed a lock of her hair, as her love shared.

6.

Each envelope higher in memory pile,
Still handwritten, with loops, with slanted word,
Their goddess's head, post office circle stamped,
Military Post, large font down the right side,
Became more distant and she so more returned.

Each letter opened wrote less about love,
More distant than they, Brighton '37,
More about the big world he was now seeing,
More about days being blues at sea,
Becoming less loving, her heart felt so spurned.

One letter she sent with no profit as its read,
The men, the neighbours, the churches so fell,
The Germans blitzing through London's core,
Buildings turned to rubble over night,

Date timed but slow to her so doormat,
Her post late to his dispatch,
King George's head to the corner,

The Luftwaffe shadowed the horrid of war.

She was in the underground for safety's sake,
He was under the sea on night surveillance.
Her letters written without truthful eyes,
His returned with no glamour or honour.
Love slowly removed since blown kissed goodbyes.

7.

In his dorm was her true stone,
Her 'ever eyes of blue stone',
Her 'written promise through stone',
A kissed round, they'd ever grow.

And on the first word he imagined her stood at the door,
As pretty as any girl he had ever met.

On first line he saw her in his mind, waving,
Under the porch, tip-toed, with an anxious smile.

Her hair, fringed, shoulder-length, curled under,

And as he saw her hand-written name and kisses,
His eyes welled to blurred vision, upset.

...

And her lock of hair under his pillow was kept.

8.

In the candlelight, reflected in the mirror,
On the mantle, closed, next to her brush,
Her memory box of blue had been locked.

She could not bear to open,
She wished she were blind,
She shivered a horrid thought,
At the envelope top of the pile.

Addressed, 12 Victoria Cottages, London Town,

The stamp, head of King George, rose and thistle,...

But, there was no *Military Post* to the right side ...

No loops to the address Ss,
No slant to the words upright,
The envelope, white, perfectly clean,
On His Majesty's Service, as the top line.

Each letter typed through a ribbon fine.

...

On the first line she imagined him struck by war,
End of the paragraph imagined where he was.
The final sentence, cold condolences for her loss.

Dated, 2nd December 1941.

His body was not found.

By the date, she counted how long he was so out there,
By the wording, he was in The Channel off the north coast,
By the signature, thought of his last letter he wrote,

Downed by a bomb off a German boat.

9.

On the end of Brighton pier, sun down, fairground closed,
Nobody on pebble beach, the children had all gone home.

She held his stone as a heart in her clasp.

She held his blue stone,
'Forever be true stone',
'Will never be through stone'.

He died with her blue stone at bunk,
He died with a curl of her hair.
He died, ... and she was not there,

To the sea, with love, her pebble be so thrown.

...

At first thought she unclasped the heart in her hand,
With arm above, behind head, second thought of love.
In waves' noise, the thought of her man in blues ...

Her thoughts of 1937,
The pier played a carousel tune,
In hand they walked as two,

... Her stone beach pebble lover, ... to the other, she threw.

....

Her love did ever so run through her wording,
The blue of stone ever reflected hope,
She always adored him,
Her arms waited here for him,
Her man of the Navy, forever be missed.

....

Back to railings she, her heart so cried.

At first tear she thought of herself dressed in white,
Through sobbing imagined her wedding veil smile,
Through heartache saw her man stood medal to chest,

Through fingers across face, thought she could so die.

The knell of the bell, was never peels for the bride.

Her mind forever remembered Brighton,
Two years before he went off to war.
Their pebble beach love started with,
And was supposed to, also end with,

One big promenade *so* vanilla kiss.

When you get to the bridge of change,
Have the strength to cross alone.

If you cannot,
It's not wrong to ask for another's hand.

Thinking Bridge

1.

When the cathedral has peeled its goodnight bell;
A deeper tone, that says all is still well,
And there is a silence over the city …

Where lights stray across the path that I have walked,
The trees shadow the pavement onto the road …

Leaf patterns across the lights are thrown …

This is my thinking bridge,
The bridge in the midnight hour.
This, where I lose sense of time,
I try to create my own peace of mind.

With spindles of black and rail of oak,
This is my crossing bridge, built bespoke.

With two elbows resting,
I have the moon as my light.
My thoughts, my reflective pose,
I always look down, thoughts surmised.

Below,
Painted are flowerpot boats,
But,
My history never goes.
Brightly moored by tether rope,
Stilled dark canal water never flows.

The cathedral bell strikes half three,
This is where I will still be …

With life's spindles twisted,

I stand alone, on neither bank.

This, the bridge crossing, for my humbled mind.

2.

Scarred, is my fallowed field,
The field of my past and now.
That has grown tall many years,
Yet others, were just so hard ploughed.

For the four fences yield no tall grains,
I stand on what I cannot explain.

This is my sallowed field,
Far from yester hallowed field.
No wind blows, no sun I feel,
No emotion shown, no smile revealed.

I stand on what I cannot explain.
My shadow from sun, is the ground's stain.

This, my field of planted seed,
That lies dormant to prouder weed,
That lies a reminder to life taint,
From four fences, I can't be freed,

To find greener pasture is my aim,
To the skeleton oak shadow, I remain.

3.

And ...

My sanity tree is no longer me,
To be part of spring blossoms, I cannot be.
For every self-month is now winter,
Every summer day is now hinter.

My grounding oak, now winter-bare,
Lost memory foliage to autumn's air.

These are my oaken leaves,
Have now become broken leaves,
Shed bare, as though token leaves,
As though my memories thieved.

They fall dried and brown to ground,
Glad memories, hold little vanity,
Are no longer to my mind's tree, bound.

Every night I search for the happy leaf,
Cast away, without any sound.
My sanity tree is no longer me,
My reminder happiness never achieved.

I desperately want good memories found.

4.

Midnight heard the tear-eyed man,
Stood again on his bridging span.

The one peel bell heard him crying,
To get to his happier place, trying.

The two peel bells heard him sobbing,
Heard, his heart and mind throbbing.

Three o clock, one man silently screamed,
His whiten fist to his teeth,
That broke dark of night's serene …

That shed his oak leaves of dreams,

That tore his mind's inner seams,
That bore his heart's inner, dying.

5.

Every night I pick up every leaf,
Look on the top, look underneath.
On every side is more disbelief,

Every held leaf, shows veins of grief.

Every night I saw my life tree of oak,
Into planks and I make them bow,
To build my mind's midnight bridge,
Taken years of work, years so slow,

Every night, to my field, I must go,
In the echo sound of the nesting crows,

With my knees to the fallow ground,
With my tears to the sallowed, drowned.
My cries hopeful to grow my own seeds,
Praying for tall grain, long ago sown.

Knelt in life's self-ploughed furrows,
My head in the many self-dug burrows,
Looking for my happier roots of life,
Looking for why … to this man I've grown.

Every leaf held, shows veins of grief.
Great sadness that I hold, on my own.

6.

My desperate weave basket I hold,
To gather memory leaves, hundred-fold.
Each with stems of dried sadness,
Each gathered in the winter's cold.

Each gathered with tears of woe,
Each gathered in the night alone,

To find the one happiness leaf,
To find a smile through all I know.

To find one acorn for renewed hope,
To hold one seed, might help me cope.

I carry the basket on hunch burden back,
I carry grief and woes' leaves, stacked,
To cross my mind bridge, the other side,

I never get there, though I've ever tried.

I'm trying to walk to the happier plain,
Where flowers surround fields of grain,
Where rivers babble to my life's tides,
Where my new-life tree holds no pain.

Each gathered in the winter's cold.
Each turned, to regain a little pride.

7.

Every night I pick up every leaf,
Look on the top, look underneath.

To every side, a little, my heart dies,
To find happiness, I forever do try,

On every side is more disbelief,
Every held leaf, shows veins of grief.

Every night my knees in self-sorrows,
Over the prouder weeds I cry and cry.

Over my fallowed life field, end is nye,

Into my shallow furrows, I could just lie,

On the skeleton oak, far from hallowed,
Hangs rope knotted from my gallows.

Into my hollowed burrow, ... I could die.

I see myself hanging with a face sallow.

8.

I'm looking over to fields of grain,
I can't quite cross ... I cannot explain.

My basket of memories are hauled
From the four-fenced fallow field
To a wide open arched bridge,
My mind imprisoned in sinking holes.

My life oak made the spindled bridge,
My fallow fields could be left to die,
My self-furrows turned to better ground,
My life-burrows filled to prevent my falls.

I can't quite cross ... I cannot explain.
I'm looking over to fields of grain.

What could be my ticket pass of cause?
What can be my toll, to great applause?
In need, one great memory in my head,
One leaf, in the rotten million hoard.

One leaf to stop my ever-nights of pain.
One leaf to make my heart smile again.

...

9.

The cathedral bell peeled at four.

No man on the bridge, stood there.

In lamplight, leaves shadowed the road.

The canal water, rippled in their glow.

Flowerpot boats with painted wares,

The city heard one man's scream,
That broke silence of autumn's dreams,
That heard the pain of his thought,
That felt his heart, tear, at its seams.

And blowing through the chill of air,
Were floating dream leaves, ... without a care.

To re-walk the steps of history
Helps to shape the pathway to your future.

The Mansions of Wycombe

The Grand Tour

1.

"Gentlemen, gentlemen !"

"Good evening my dear fellows;
To my parliamentarians,
To my fellow Et-o-nians,
To dearest hist-or-ians,
To closest theo-lo-gians.

With glasses to hand,
With goblets risen,
With chalice holden,

A claret Mediterranean.

Gentlemen, gentlemen !

(Oh, I forgot ...)

To my fellow vintners. (*Ha-ha*)

Let the joviality begin !"

...

And so all friends mentored,
From England's upper classes,

Within the dark of cave,
Within candlelight glow,
With fayre to the table,

Each and all raised their glasses ...

2.

"And now is the time to join in."

"Dance, dance, sing, sing,
Within our dark cave
We can do our own thing.

Dance, dance, sing, sing,
Breast of the pheasant,
Apple head of the pig.

Dance, dance, sing, sing,
The hair of the dog
Is a nose to the Whigs.

Sing, sing, drink, drink,
The vintners' red
Is the ring of the king."

"Aaa-haa-haa-haa-haa-haa-haa-haa."

...

Through hours of joviality,
Came a whole night of frivolity.

The men of such a privileged class,
Became more drunk through flagon and flask.

Slovenly leant with their seat backs lurched,

Drips to their whisker,
Claret to their shirts,

Then came the drunken stories, from the dirt ...

"Francis, Francis – do a story, to us tell,
That you have told two score times,
Where you travelled to Europe,
On your Grand Tour after Eton,

Do tell us the story, that hasn't yet been beaten."

3.

"Gentlemen, gentlemen,
So be quiet, seated and settled.
I will tell the story of younger year,
With spirit and body of finer fettle.

Gentlemen, gentlemen,
They call me a pompous, prodigal gent,
Who sees womanising, drinking and
Merriment, as money that's well spent !

I dare say that I don't blame them,
But to tell of my spendthrift years,
With my discourtesy to my money,
To tell those with a dearth, would shame fears.

Gentlemen, gentlemen,
By ship, by coach, by my steed four horses,
I wrote of my Grand Tour over the land,
As gifted to the poorer man, ...

Not just to further their small knowledge,

But a relish to tell of my wit and draw their 'plause.

I dare say that I don't blame them.
By wealth from my father inherited,
Money made from a trade of silken cloth.

Every tuppence from book sales,
Is money from the lesser fledged,

As I stand as advocate to the best of my tours."

...

But opposition was the membership of Whigs,
Who thought of Francis, and his cave brethren,
As a posh band, of the worst of the prigs.

4.

"My coach stopped in Paris,
(They call it Paree,)
With Catholics praying,
Cathedrals by The Seine,
(- they call it Senn,)
For a many a week, there I remained.

I would open my inn window.
On the cobbles down below,
Were the prettiest ladies,
Selling apples from carts, delicious their names.

Flirtatious was my nature,
Pretending apples to buy,
The prettiest of ladies,
With smile to my eyes, I asked of their game.

Oh yes !

With white lace to their ankles,
Woven from the French mills,
Lips of red, lashes were curled,

They really were the beautiful of girls!

By night I supped and supped,
Red wine from Paree chalk hills,
At inns for gentlemen only.
Wine excelled madam's wonderful breasts !

(Oh, I'm sorry,)

I meant to say, madam's hair of blacken twirls."

"Aaa-haa-haa-haa-haa-haa-haa-haa."

"The ladies with ginormous boobies,
From tightened corset and strings,
Were the largest of import fruits,
I needed to untie the whole bloody thing !'

"Aaa-haa-haa-haa-haa-haa-haa-haa."

...

The Whigs fought against the related monarchy,
(Who sided with Vintners to their loan,)
To detest the Tories through protest and anarchy.

...

5.

"Quiet, oh quiet gentlemen,
Let your ears and glasses be settled.
So next I tell of a stinking dockside,
Where women were never God-petalled,

Horses were running tired,
We stopped at Bordeaux town,
The drudgery of the port side,
However, for days we would reside.

My character of love was
Instantly tamed temper,
The ladies with no teeth bore,

(And equal to dogs with distemper,)

Each one a dis-charming lanterned whore !

It wasn't so much their selling,
But of the dirt to clothes,
Also their bodily wears,

... And their facially explicit hairs !"

"Aaa-haa-haa-haa-haa-haa-haa-haa."

"Docking of sailors and barrels,
Merchandise landed from south Spain,
Brought disgust to this whole place,

(My britches so firmed by strapped brace,)

But we did buy labelled red by the case!

Bottle by bottle downed,
By night I supped and supped,
Sat on the dockside barrels,

(The lantern-side lady seemed better,)

My gentleman's ego suddenly looked up !

The whore, paid, was then unfettered,
Within the wharf-side buildings.
Madam's white bloomers leased ...

What was good for me, was the same for the priest!"

"Aaa-haa-haa-haa-haa-haa-haa-haa."

6.

Through hours of telling stories,
Came the exaggeration in all glory.

The men of such a privileged school,
Became more drunk, and so more the fool.

Heads to tables, hands to drink, bottoms to stools.

Stains to their shirts,
Claret-wet, their britches.

Then came more drunken stories, from his mirth.

7.

"My loins in britches, wide of girth,
My coach rested in Naples,
Where streets are of narrowness,
And the bay vast to the eye view.

Above inns below, laundry hung,
Sign to the ladies selling,
Where my eyes were wide divide,
The tiny houses couldn't bed two.

I met a lady artist with brush
In the bite of her whiten teeth,
Black smock over her pretty frock,
Made my mind think what was underneath.

Gentlemen, gentlemen, fellows,
Delicious red from near Rome,
By night, I supped and supped.
The lady artist showed me her home!"

"Aaa-haa-haa-haa-haa-haa-haa-haa."

"I asked of her artistic talent,
As she lay there on whiten cotton.
Would she like to go back to nature,

With dress, corset and stocking forgotten ?!"

"Aaa haa haa haa haa haa haa haa"

"And if thought be ground was shaken by Vesuvius,
I would question if your mind should be so dubious.

Gentlemen, gentlemen,
Compliments were proliferated,
So shy were the ladies I did meet.

(I dare say I don't blame them),

With mark-ed score, I should be so elated!"

8.

"Florence was red tiles, Catholics and domas,
Their religion was a love of statues.
One thousand churches in one thousand streets,
Every hour could be prayer time in a retreat !

The ladies sold grapes from wooden cart,
With a bosom so much fairer than others,
I forgot the laced ladies from Paree,
The pretties from Florence I would so marry !

But now's the time I acknowledge the sinner,
My words used to elicit her smile,
A goddess, was she, with hair to seduce,
She would be mine, by rhetoric or rouse.

After ladies, art and my dinner,
My horse tethered by gentlemen's inn,
The native red under lanterned light,
By dark of night I supped and supped."

"Aaa-haa-haa-haa-haa-haa-haa-haa."

"Not all statues were crafted women fair,
Not all art was as brush to a canvas,
But my two eyes, in Florence, were so averted,
By the statue of David, his britches deserted!"

"Aaa-haa-haa-haa-haa-haa-haa-haa."

9.

"With Temple Acropolis to the hill,
And pillars still lined cobbled street,
Athens of Greece was my final haunt,
My character of love was still to flaunt.

The ladies sold olives from rolling cart,
With their mothers, four feet, were so short,
The beauties of young were really daughters ?
Smiling goddesses, my mind was taunt.

Goddesses they were between ancient pillars,

Goddesses they were ...

(Oh, my !)

But my taste buds went from fond to dower;
She fed me cheese, to my lips to please ...

She fed me native olives, one by one,
Each fed to my mouth with her gorgeous smi-ile.

I tasted hon-ey from the Greek forests,
Like nothing I've ev-er tasted before ...

But our love lock was then so heartbroken,
Their local wine tasted of vinegar, soured !"

"Aaa-haa-haa-haa-haa-haa-haa-haa."

10.

"Gentlemen, gentlemen,

Solitude was never to be my intention,
Love on tour was the my great re-invention,
But Francis of Dashwood would never so
Be the man, of everyday conven-tion.

Gentlemen, gentlemen,

It was in the Vatican that, for my own thought,
I was banned on my lack of retort.
My hands and mind, not so reverend,
The Pope and his bishops held me to court !

I dare say I don't blame them ...

They saw me as though forever sinning,
Through my promiscuous side to women.

But I return the blame, also to them ...

They also like the women of white, lacen hem !

Gentlemen, Gentlemen,

Fellow Hell-Fire Club members,
I tell you this to ever remember ...

Money on women is well spent,
As they are so heavenly-sent.

But, (ha-ha),

Never drink too much Mediterranean red,
Before picking the lady you want in your bed !

Although by day they are selling fruit from carts,
By night, with my rhetoric and my rouse,
With too much of the local booze,

(I couldn't elicit a thought in trouser),

They all seemed a bunch of brazen tarts!"

"Aaa-haa-haa-haa-haa-haa-haa-haa."

The Silver Spoon

I knew not that she'd be familiar,
To the pages of my writing.
A 'by chance' to later meeting,
Would become more than a friendly greeting ...

1. Winter's Freeze

December's dark of wintered trees,
Port wine over crackling warmed,
Cloves dried and cinnamon sticks,
Lanterns lit 'side a blazing logged fire.

January's cold saw the harshest snow,
Written quill in hue of glowing.
Ink welled by oaken boxed notes,
The hand of author, writes his desire.

February's month showed deepened frost,
Another letter from my queen.
She reminded, that it be primrose month,
The deaden hedgerows covert the sire.

...

I must walk February woodland in cold,
For first shoots past whiten frost.
If trees be thought as nature's church,
The yellow petals, are the singing choir.

...

Past mistletoe bowed for Christmas kisses,
Holly was bird winter staple,
No more acorns, squirrels forage,
The deaden of ground, beyond fenced wire.

A reminder gifted from Osborne's queen,
Five petal hearts break Hughenden's wintry scene.

2. Faery Queen

To her command, I meet the widow queen,
As her prime minister, to protocol, I bestow.
As I entered and offered the lowest bow,
As room broke from a pageanted serene ...

She drank to our love.
She was Verdi's Violetta.

I heard everyone will consume our pleasure,
I heard how love, be a fleeting moment,
I heard, love is a flower, that never fades,
My Faery Queen, was my heart's treasure.

She enacted Verdi's Violetta,
She drank to they above.
From hence forth,
For years coming,
I would be at ... my Faery Queen's pleasure.

3. Of Cloak or Dagger

Should you ask if I be man
Of cloak, or of dagger,
I would answer as "both" –
Parliament-ary is the cloak,
With linguistical drawn dagger.

Should you ask If I be man
Of hope, or of a fear,
(Hmmm)
I would answer as ... "both" –
Man should have heart of every hope,
But know the fear of greasy rope.

Should you ask if, ... I be man ...
Of feast, or of famine ?
(Well Sir)
I would answer ... "they both" –
One should know meaning of famine,
To know your feast, of any least.

Should you ask If I be man
Of strength, or of courage,
(*Ha-ha*)
Considered thought ... "both" –
One needs for courage, his strengths;
His mind, his heart, his arm, his legs.

...

Yet,
Should you ask if I married
For love ... or for mon-ey ?
(Good Sir !)

I would answer with a thumb under brace ...

Money cushioned in her breast,
Will do well, to line my box chest.

Just as manor bees grant me honey,
I married for love – *of* – her money !

...

When a good true friend died,
His widow he bequeathed.
For the sake of them both –
And truth, isn't so flowery,
I had, Sir,
One hand to heart, one to her dowry.

My indebted past, isn't so flowery,
I can now stand as gentry,
I can now stand on land,
I can now stand for parliament ...

One hand on heart, one on her dowry !

....

Should you ask if I be man
Of friend, or of a foe,
I would answer, Madam, "neither" –
To befriend can embattle cause,
No foe receiveth vote nor 'plause.

4. The Posey

One foot forward with pointed shoe,
One leg almost kneeled back to floor,
One hold of Her Majesty's right hand,
A kiss to her glove, showed his adore.

Compliments often flatter,
With written quill and waxen seals,
With having friendship, he wrote her need,
She, seated to throne, he made common law.

And she offered a bow of primroses,
Touching tips, a friendship posey,
Given to no man since her Albert died,

With five petal hearts, could it mean more ?

A friendship with her lower class,
No etiquette, in her royalty law ...

With five petal hearts within her posey,

If Dizzy, were not a married man,
Could it really mean, a whole lot more ?

A kiss to her glove, showed his adore.

5. The Regale

The dandy young fellow of society,
A character to match his wit.
With moustache so long and twisted,
With his oiled black hair curls,
With his change of religion,
For the parliament, this man should now sit.

And now

His regale is of a feathered fortune nest,
Peacocks display a proud pleasance.
His leg higher in polish boot,
His britches of cloth, cut to suit.
His stable, its own stallion,
He's riding high, above common peasant.

Two silvered links hold cuffs,
One pair of bone spectacles,
One chain fob to pocket,
One silvered pin makes present.

Beyond my credentials they have not reckoned,
With a twist of wit, and of thought,
Their opposition, be blunted, in a second.

6. Betrothal

When she giveth primroses, bowed,
I kissed the five love heart petals,
As I might, to forehead of born child.
My love for Her Majesty, was bestowed.

My thought of friendship and of queen,
My consensual hand, so betrothed.

Could the primroses that I begot,
Be renamed forget-me-nots ?

The very nature of this man,
Be, to covert his master's plans.
Sir,
Beyond, those many five petals,
To her tea table, my feet be settled.

7. Tally One

Two thousand honey bees,
Two score of blacky cattle,
One brace of whiten swans,
Two brace of peacocks please.

And

One stallion for breeding,
Four mares of blacky rumps,
Twenty brace of pheasants,
Four sucking pigs, killed for freeze.

8. Bookmarks

Her Majesty's primroses are dried and pressed,
Testament of our remembered times.
Until we mighten to meet again,
They decor the page marker, to my storied lines.

To Osborne House, by first class steed post, I had her sent,
Engiftment of yellow posies were pressed,
So she could slip them in royal ledger,
To Regina Victoria, they be addressed.

...

Our flower of friendship,
Doest last more than the weeks six.
Pressed, with my regards,
By my fair hand, they were picked.

9. One Nation

From notorietied family of wealth,
We came to country for my health.

I stand rear of manor looking south,
Across the Wye's green-treed valley.

A thought of the split-classed country,
A thought through pipe, of a one nation,
A thought working classes cast their say,
Against bigoted bosses, let them rally.

Sir,
Create this country, to generate wealth,
To flatter Her Highness, is ultimate stealth.

10. Tally Two

Parliamentarians against *myself*, did rally,
Knowing my indebtedness in scores.
Plastered to my Commons seat,
They deplore I should settle my tally.

Seven house staff need paying,
Four indebted grants to The Manor,
Two merchants bills for cheese,
One to church pocket, for praying.

My avoidance of me paying ...
Is the reason ... I am praying !

Opposition point and shout across royal mace,
While slamming the oak judgement gabble.
With my creditors I might haggle,
I'm Prime Minister ! Recognise this face !

If I were a mere commoner ...
I'd be gaoled without a trace.

11. December Luncheon

Mid-December, by the prime minister's request,
The monarch to attend the Manor of Hughenden.
The invite with parliamentary decree,
He to prepare luncheon, fit for a queen.

This was the time to oil his curls,
His britches also cut as pristine.

Pulled into the station, the locomotive of steam,
One step helped by the hand of Disraeli,
One bow to kiss the glove that lifts,
One posey of primroses, she gave as gift.

And so she came to The Manor's wrought gates,
Ornate in curves, by which his keepers wait.

Following five furlongs of limes,
In the late morning scene,
Two footmen, four horses,
One carriage, one queen.

To help her down from the carriage,
His steeds ran front of hers.
Flattery to grace the monarch of reign,
He greeted his Vickie, yet again.

Twisted, were the ten chairs of oaken.
In the mid-lunchtime scene;
Eight guests, four candles,
Three courses, one queen.

Further to lunch, gents reside,
Smoking jackets of velvet, dark.
To flatter queen, yet once again,
Of clay pipe party, he refrains.

With claret on his oiled curls,
The queen wore a necklace, pearled.

Patterned were the chaise-longe to retire.
In Hughenden's drawing room scene;
Two sofas, one Dizzy,
One honoured ... by the presence ... of one's Queen.

12. The Silver Spoon

Indebtedness removed from mouth the silver spoon,

To its replacement could never be too soon.

My queen allowed me to taste the sugar more so sure,
By my wanten to serve, by her wanten allure.

Testament lies across the letherned green desk,
Written entitlement, made higher, by her request.

All deeds and seals, are of quill and squid ink pure,
Still held in esteem, costumed, for minds to endure.

Where Russians sat higher with titles to impress,
In statute law, She became first India Empress.

Friendship and sugar acquainted our lovely esteem,
Here to die ... for my country ... and *before* My Queen.

Dear fellows,
Call me a radical or Victorian boon,
I tasted many tainted ... *and* silver spoons.

13. Love and Regret

Springtime's light of the blossomed trees,
The smell of temperance rains,
The beauty of birdcall, and bound of the hare,
Ran long past the savaged winter's airs.

Flooded will be meadows with wild flower,
Wind be softer through the long grasses,
To awaken the workforce of manor bees,
Season of mating, nature's loves do pair.

Through illness, I feel the ending of my time,
Through every word, thoughts meander.
Through every love, dreams have considered,
Thoughts of regret, slough my heart embittered.

Ne'r write acrimonious to ever offend,
Compliment with love, words and a smile.
From their memory, never will you so fade,
Selfish heart held, be love that's been frittered.

....

Dearest Victoria,
Should you ask if I be man
Of love, or of regret,
(*Cough*)
I would answer "both" –
Love happens many a way, so unasked,
Regret, is all love I held back, never ... unmasked.

...

I heard my lone steps in Westminster's halls,
My lone shadow across parliament's walls,
My lone gown flowing along corridors,
Each tiny battle to win the greater wars.

Her portrait hung from the walls of stone,
Beyond darkest doors, I'd never be alone.

...

My dearest Faery Queen,
If asked whether a primrose lady
For love or friendship ?
You would answer "both" –
Friendship is congenial and common shared.
Love lies within any two friends, laid bare.

14. The Funeral

Upon the day for beloved Disraeli,
Upon his coffin laid a primrose wreath,
Upon laid such simple words to paper,
"His favourite flowers" written in grief.

To know they came out of such good friends,
To know words of little emotion,
And to know Victoria could not attend,
To cry for the man, of given devotion.

Four days later by royal request,
Victoria came where he laid in rest.

Through Buckinghamshire's beeches ...
Four blackened rump horses,
Two footmen to their reigns,
One blackened hood carriage,
One blackened friend, in blackened veil.

Five furlongs of drive up to The Manor,
Three scores of avenued lime trees,
Four blackened horses on slow reign,
For love, Victoria came back again.

You could hear the silence in the flint church,
Her gift, his name, never be besmirched.

One hundred tears, as her head lowed,
Ten fives of petal hearts show grief,
Two score minutes restless horses wait,

To the memory of her Disraeli, of late.

15.

The spring primroses of March,
Had now flowered and died.
T'was May, Benjamin passed away.
They too, seemly empathised.

16.

She became Puccini's Cio Cio San,
She cried to see her Dizzy again,
She cried to see him off Osborne's,
She cried he might climb The Manor hill.
In hope, she would so, forever wait.

She cried, primroses in hand.
Maybe, ... one beautiful day ...

Never would she so understand.

17.

The primrose remembered in bequest,
A long thought after, he layeth to rest.

...

18.

Thirteen decades plus later,
We came to run through three scores of limes.
We came to sit atop Hughenden's hill.
We came to stand on Disraeli's terrace.

The man of opposition, became a man much greater.

To the honour of Benjamin,
Swathes of tulips kissed his parkland,
Bunches of daffodils sire the trees,
Buttercups rolled down Hughenden's hill.

Putting Tories centre ground, made Britain's path much straighter.

We touched trees through which Victoria rode,
We saw her crying through the flint church pews,
We imagined her sat looking over the valley,
And marvelled the marbled friendship words.

...

On this, such a beautiful day.

To walk bare foot is freedom.
Laces are the ties of armies
Fighting for the very same.

Walk your freedom.

Barbados Skies

I'm looking out to distant skies,

Recalling years, that have passed me by.

I'm walking slow on childhood sands,

I crush golden grains through my hands.

The palm trees, much taller than me,
I want their view, as they look out to the sea.
Heads held high with branches of greens,
I want to feel breeze, humid through leaves.

I want to feel ease, as though I'm free.

White-sailed boats that bob in seas,
Are my karma of mind, they are there to please.
To rock in breezes all the day long,
Percussion waves lap, to my life's song.

Cream parasols, lining my view,
Stretching finger to finger, stand in twos;
Pyramids, for the pharaohs below,
Are shading the embalmed, head to toe.

Sails that sit on the sea, curved,
Are fruit slices, to blue martini served.
White hemming clouds to the sea's splice,
Are white frosted sugar to sweeten the ice.

I can taste the fruit
On my martini …
It tastes so nice.

Greyer storm clouds are in a rush,

Stroked through the sky from the artist's brush.

Sea birds, V shapes 'bove the waves,

The italic signature he engraved.

2. Red Heart Tree

If ever you should dance with me,
You would wear a chain from the flamboyant tree.

I danced alone along the beach,
With a whisper of song in the breeze.
My image waltzing with arms around you,
A glimpse of light through the trees.

My heart glowed like a sunset night,
As I stood to the lapping shores.
Wanting to grab the light atop the mast,
And bring it, to make it yours.

In the dark I saw a glow of red,
The heavens shone from above.
I collected flowers from flamboyant tree,
To bring you a handful of love.

Overwhelming thought, a tree for two,
There's a flower for every kiss,
The red of desire, that says everything love,
Each petal, moments, reminisced.

I imagined that we stood on
the shore, with a wedding made for two.
Wear a chain of hearts, from flamboyant tree,
As a sign of my ever love for you.

If ever I were to marry thee,
You would wear a chain from the red heart tree.

3. Cocktail Skies

The lovers held hands and thoughts on the beach,
From a hue of yellow, they became red silhouettes.
The white yachts glided home, their harbour a haven,
Winged birds cut coloured sky, back to their nests.

We sat and watched Barbados sky close for the night,
Late afternoon sand was a mess, from days of play.
Crabs side-lined on rocks, battered by waves,
The galleon stood upright, anchored to the bay.

The ocean, a giant quilt, white lines on blue,
We saw the sun's thoughts, as he lowed to bed;
Whilst counting puff ball clouds, from right to left,
His colourful dreams were orange, yellow and red.

...

The galleon was the tall stirrer in the ocean glass,

As we drank in the rum cocktail-layered sky.

The palm tree straws stood tall in the edge view,

Behind ice cube rocks, paper boats passed by.

4. Tropical Rains

The clouds were cumulus thrones on seas,
Where gods could sit, drinking dark rum tea ...

The Caribbean storm thundered the night,
Rain pelted pavements and roofs.
From fond dreams of Barbados skies,
To lightning that showed cries of fright.

The tropical rains were cooling the air,
The monsoon month, where heavens cry.
Lullaby frog song that shrilled through dark,
Now remained silent, in the storm's mare.

Torrid were the tides,
As rains wouldn't abide.

The rumble of thunder that broke our nights,
Pitted the beach, where we once walked.
From the empathy moon, that half-smiled,
To the scorn of the storm, the hate it incites.

Hold me much tighter to protect me the most,
Sheets to chins cover our souls,
The storm is knocking, at window panes,
It's not invited, and we're not its host.

Horrid were our dreams,
As light, through glass streamed.

5. The Morning

All was quiet after the nights of storm,
Shutters were opened to meet the dawn.
Smell the sea at the tide's edge,
Fine weather, here again, has made its pledge.

Palms that bowed away from the coast,
Stood upright, arms wide, to greet the host,
The dawn rose as picture skies,
And put turquoise colour back to tides.

Boat keels bob to acknowledge our show,
Side to side masts, wave, as to say hello.
Bell weather friends start our day,
Receding grey skies surround the bay.

Wet was the sand along the bay,
As the tide still cried itself away.

Black men, bare foot, groomed battered sand,
With long-tined rakes, to their hands.
They dismiss the storm's nightly rages,
As sun to faces, white smiles engaging.

Footprints show I had walked the sands,
Palm trees' shadows were holding hands.

...

The sun lounger clouds that hemmed the bay,
Predicted calm for the rest of the day.

6. Hat of Straw

I'm looking under brimmed hat of straw,
Thinking nothing, like the nothing before.

It's hard to believe there are wars,
In countries beyond that horizon,
Where religions battle under the same sky,
We can see, but not understand why.

And the tabloid papers can just go away,
Their stench of news make minds decay.

It's hard to believe people still starve,
In nations beyond what I can see.
Dictators control with their stripes of rank,
Yet we give to their governing bank.

And yesterday's news is not my today,
I need sun, not headlines, in my way.

It's hard to believe there's no water,
In far villages, as hot as this day,
Where babies' mouths cry of dehydration,
Yet others can wash, the whole of a nation.

Let the papers prospect, MPs their prey,
My headphones in, there is nothing to say.

And it's harder to believe I don't believe,
As I live this Bajan island's life.
The locals sit on a rock, patience waits,
The fish net catching, dinner for plates.

I'm looking outwards with a concaved sky,
With brim-shaded eyes, I'm a could be a spy.

7. The Galleon of Hope

The galleon that moored in the bay,
Would be mine on another day ...

I've thought of my life as on a ship,
From the crests of waves to the troughs I could dip.
When winning, dark rum I would sip,
When losing, my shirt's sleeves would be stripped.

Off front deck, I would cast life's net,
It would be hauled in, to see the catch I'd fetched,
I never thought of my net having holes,
But of binding strong rope, to hold all my goals.

I'd always collect new found bounty,
Sailing life's rugged shoreline, county to county.
Lighthouses were my first warnings,
Preferring to dock, in the love of your moorings.

I would climb the mast to crow's nest,
Optimistically thinking, high view would be best.
Mine was the olive branch from the dove,
He's showing there's land 'hoy, and gods were above,

...

So I cast my net to midnight sky,
Knowing what I caught, would be mine.
My hope was to catch as many stars,
But luck caught me love, ... Venus and Mars.

I followed the wisdom mast by night,
Morning Star last, in the early light.
My love still glows, in all the same,
Gods tell it's Venus, from where you came.

Now I know my ship is moored,
My nets folded, I'm finally yours.

...

We slowly walk the beach of content,
Moments on it, together spent.
We sit and ponder on lovers' sand,
Bare foot thoughts, ... sandals in hands.

...

The galleon that moored in the bay,
Has found the best ever place, here to stay.

8. Couples' Beach

Puffing clouds follow the distant sea line,
As if the Bajan train, had just passed by.

Take a stroll along couples' beach,
Where lovers walk, under Bajan skies.
Softer sand to turquoise blue,
That's where I held my love, so true.

We picked red petal flowers,
Where lovers walk, under Bajan skies.
They blew in breeze to the sea;
Love hearts from the flamboyant tree.

We looked into the darkest night,
Where lovers walk, under Bajan skies.
The whistling frog in the tree,
The highest descant to you and me.

...

Lovers walk under Bajan skies,

Because romance runs through Bajan tides,

The whole world can run besides,

As Barbados is, ... about you and I.

...

Looking through Barbados skies,
We lost thoughts of our real lives.

9. Sandals In Hand

This is a walk for my own thoughts,
Along the beach, ... sandals in hand.
The clouds are thrones for the gods,
Where there are none of life's demands.

We're feeling breeze through our hair,
Along the beach, ... sandals in hand.
With few words, but our hands we share,
We are walking slow with nothing planned.

And we could still see the galleon in the bay,
The light on the mast, glowed the main stay.

We're feeling coolness on our soles,
Along the beach, ... sandals in hand.
The hottest of days, melted the ice,
Refreshing thoughts, and skin so tanned.

Footprints for two, each one of them our thoughts,
Heading the same direction, ... wanten to explore.

10. The Mermaid

There I saw you, as my beautiful mermaid,
Drying in sunlight, as though you swam from the bay.
Your hair splayed across golden sands,
Your loveliness shone from head to waist.

I took the hand, of my beautiful mermaid,
I kissed your shoulder and tasted skin oil,
Lips passing, slowly, down to your wrist,

The taste of sea salt, my lover loyal.

To taste sea salt rubbed with oil.

I walk on sand, with my beautiful mermaid,
Leading back on tides, to your turquoise home,
We swim in two, through the sea's waves,
Over proud pink corals, we lovers can roam.

...

My beautiful mermaid, smile for me,
You are my princess, from ocean dreams.
Will you say that you'll marry me ?
We can live together in turquoise seas.

...

I know you wear my turquoise ring,
That does match the colour, where you swim.

11. The Tide Line

My late dearest father, how could I forget,
My childhood memories that are on the beach.
I want to tell about Barbados,
Times missed, is my regret.

I followed your footprints for so long,
Impressions that helped me understand.
I looked back, for reassurance,
As the tide lowed, they were gone.

Emptiness is a beach with a hollow shell,
The tide line defines our family time,
Sand castles that were our fortress,
Are now the flats, where they fell.

...

I want to tell you we both had a good time,
I want to remember you were also here.
You saw then, the same Bajan skies ...

Your past Barbados ... is now mine.

12. Turtle Beach

At the turn of ten, we walked again to the beach,
Where sun beds slept with shades blocking the stars.
Hand held in hand and footprints then followed,
We sat on the shoreline to wait long for tomorrow.

The percussion waves that never ever will sleep,
Came to greet as disciples, to again recede.
Our trail of prints paralleled in evening balm,
Were washed away, again, to leave sands of calm.

We remembered our day as we laid on the sea,
Snorkelling for two, heads look downwards to view.
Sunlight through ripples, patterned across sands,
Angel fish tails shimmer as though litten fans.

Turquoise streaks transed through a universe of light,
Flotsom clung mid-water to eventually meet shore.
Parrot fish vogued in makeup, as princesses grand,
Eels protect rock holes, as turrets be manned.

There you shimmer as a mermaid in bluest water,
Corals adore you, with lady fishes-in-waiting.
A vision, though heaven-sent, in shell-crested light,
Angels of Neptune would swoop, to dart out of sight.

From restaurants in shoes, to bare feet in sand,
I turned up my leggings, water through toes.
From days where tourist boats, would embark,
I thought of us sailing from water dark, into dark.

So, we sat in lanterned light on the turtle beach,
Where hornbills come to nest their hatch in the night.
We remember lost love ones, as stars in the sky,
They're winking at us, after our long past goodbyes.

As we stared into the night sky, in late hours,
We promised the sparkler comet was ours.

We told stories in darkness, from our history past,
The pleasure of remembrance, shared with you.
Glass of Merlot, a trophy, in nestling fingers,
Recalling, in the silence, how the best ones linger.

....

The light glimpsed from behind, to point to the shore,
And, as though a star had fallen from the night skies,
It settled on a silhouette with one knee in sand,
He made his proposal, diamond ring to her hand.

And the wooden galleon cut into the night sky,

Little boats became a midnight-lit pageant.

The Milky Way played a star-dotted sonata,

The fat lady sang finale for the operetta.

The whole world can run besides,
As Barbados is, ... about you and I.

13. Reflections

Goodbye Barbados !

I threw my hat to the blue sea,
A gift to Barbados,
That they will ever be free.

The Bajan sun didn't agree,
And returned my straw hat,
On the sea's breeze to me.

I recalled in reflecting mind,
The island's beauty that I find ...

Warmer breezes,
Darker skies,
Insects' chorus,
Sunset tides.
Coloured chatelle,
Boarded walls,
Taller palms,
Whistle frog calls.
Curving beaches,
Sand-lined views,
Bajan living,
Love to you.
Polite smiles,
Loving eyes,
Happy to help,
Contented pride.

Goodbye Barbados,
It has been a pleasure,
You've won my heart,
You're the ocean's treasure.

And the whole world can run besides,
As Barbados ... it's about you and I.

14. Chatelle For Two

We nailed our house name to wood,
The chatelle, was just me and you.
Snipped the ribbon to the island,
Our dreams of Bajan had come true.

We opened the slat shutters,
And felt breezes from sea blue.
We dreamt the skies of Barbados,
At sunset ... it was just us ... we two.

We had stood on the lovers' beach,
Picked a colour from the sky,
And found our blue turquoise chatelle,
Light transed, cream wood-slatted blinds.

With found driftwood for sideboards,
Love-laced bed, for our home,
We saluted Barbados bubbles,
Reminded ourselves, the best to come.

Oh Barbados, I can't ever be free.

I left and adored you.

My picture postcards,
As two turtle doves,
Kept safe in a blue box,
And labelled with love.

It's my secret box.

Again, and yet again,
Your beaches I kissed,
I looked back on life,
It was they, that I missed.

Oh Barbados, your sand beaches are me,
For walkers of life, where dreams are free.

...

We opened the door to meet cool,
The ceiling fan whirled a breeze.
Our memories left in the hallway,
Paired sandals, were our stress free.

...

Oh Barbados, your skies I must see,
For poets of life, they are lovers' dreams.

Oh Barbados, we can never be free,
Our Bajan love affair ... is just us three.

...

Two handfuls of love
We threw into the tides;
Red heart tree flowers,
To say our goodbyes. x.

Every step down the aisle to altar
Is a conscientious step;
Each treads the past, the now, the future;

The falls, the joys and each love lost.

And there is a hand waiting,
Waiting to share every moment.

The Wedding

The Dream

Through the cold of the night,
We both took to fly.

Can you hear his mighty wings?

I saw you behind, riding pillion,
On the back of a pure white stallion.

Pegasus flew into the starred sky.
We sat between his feathered wings.

We could hear the air pushed down.

In thought, the world was to be ours,
Through sleeping hours, of no other sound.

...

To the spring moon we both flew,
Stars lit the night sky through.

...

I looked to see you riding pillion,
To realise we were just one of dream-struck millions.

Every Pegasus that flew that night,
One pace forward with flap of wings.
Negativity would be to look down.
In thought, universe could be theirs,
They flew high from the safeness of ground.

The night flight was of the dreaming millions,
Where stars dotted the sky in zillions.

Can you hear their mighty wings?

...

Dreams should be shared, to make them come true,
Your dreams are mine, they are made for us two ...

Teasels stand sun-kissed in morning dew,
A meadow of rays, yellow, highlight through.
Thistle tops are drowned, on bad hair day,
Cobwebs stretch, as trampolines of play.

Where nightingales hover in blue skies,
Silhouetted, as the sun shines behind.
Summer hares kick-run the corn field's edge,
Purple brambles cascade the meadow's hedge.

Looking on summer nights to open skies,
We can behold and see the heaven's eyes.
And our god's monocle is the full moon,
We laughed as though he was spying us two.

Our dreams consuming the mountain top view,
Love edelweiss stands after, the snow melts through.

Ice cubes are diamonds in life's glass,
The ever-cocktail, shouldn't be drunk so fast.
Your lips are kissing its gold painted rim,
That will match perfect, the colour of your ring.

And the summer fields sing our love's song,
With hands held, nothing can ever be wrong.
Our Tudor bed grows our millionth rose,
That blossoms our dream ... to fragrant our nose.

Love-colour starfish that sleep on the sea's sand,
Are Neptune's heaven, touched by our hands.
Jellyfish lights that fly through dark blue,
Are ocean spaceships with fishes as crew.

Our dreams magnified in hope to come true,
Pillows shared in night's world, made for two.

...

Yuletide glitter glistens on our spruce tree,
On every branch is a bowed memory.
Ribboned-boxes are offerings from heart,
Your Christmas smile over a champagne flute glass.

We sit in our blue spruce tree.

Every needle is a minute.

Every pinecone a day.

Each branch is a month.

The star shines the ever years.

We sit in our blue spruce tree,
Watching year upon years,
Lit by the lights for fairies,
Tied by gold-ribbon happiness.

Can you hear his mighty wings ?

2.

Blue diamonds of harden frost,
Lie on soft snow after champagne showers.

Hear the crunch of the white snow sheet,
That lain beneath our bedtime feet.
Walking through the night of bright stars,
In hope that heaven could ever be ours.

Silhouetted, trees of night,
Stand as ghosts affront the moonlight too.

Hear the hoot of the virgin owl,
That tops the tree as a cowl.
His blink of eyes, us he views,
His lullaby sounds the whole night through.

Constellations light the sky,
A zillion stars, no space to spare.

Hear the snowy fox's winter bark,
His frozen breath mists through dark.
Nosing upward into the cold air,
Nostrils are blowing, outward they flare.

Gardens are patchwork in dark,
Plants and trees captured in pens.

Hear the arched black cat's mew,
Upon the fence for all to view.
Back's hairs of fright stand on end,
White eyes to dark, as she defends.

We know where the night sky starts,
Nobody knows where the universe ends.

3.

Platinum hooves over emerald fields,
To our airborne freedom we both ride.
Glitter trails from his flying heels,
Our Pegasus foal flies to our side.

With garnet eyes studding his virgin face,
They light our way to starlit heaven,
Where we follow the pathway of our love;
The rainbow trail through life's prism.

Mighty wings splay giant whiten feathers,
They are wafting the night sky's air;
Magnificent quills, on sheer arch blades,
The force of strength blows 'way your hair.

Moonstone mountains,
Candy floss clouds,
Through god-blown wind,
We ride Pegasus proud.

Pearls of colour line his back-laying ears,
That I hold, to heaven he strides.
They are giant shells from the sea bed,
I'm your groom, and you'll be my bride.

To his sturdy neck is a heart of flowers,
Tudor garden roses, velvet red,
With love-shape petals, white edelweiss through,
To scatter on our marital bed.

His tail holds the train of your lacen dress,
Studded with pearls through silken thread,
Hair optics of fibre glow in dark,
Pegasus is the stallion of the purest bred.

The diamond eclipse
Is your solitaire ring,
Magnified so brightly,
As the smile you bring.

Can you hear his mighty wings ?

We sat in hand on Orion's Belt.

We swam in the pan of Ursula Major.

We made love on the ribbon Milky Way.

We smiled at our full monocle moon.

Our dreams that are made for us two,
Through the night, should never end so soon.

4.

Platinum hooves land at Heaven's gate,
Where both of us must now alight.
Oak doors that have the highest arches,
White marble, the tallest read pillars.
Last steps for the dreaming lovers.

I hold you in arms to cross the threshold,
Where sunrays light our pathway.
The colosseum of the ever life,
Pantheon with the largest of domes,
The acropolis for dream-fed lovers,

Our entrance to make us both, man and wife.

....

You are draping in my holdened love.

Your bodice is of embroidered pearls.

Your waist of silken thread gathered.

Your skirt is hemming your ankles.

And your teardrop train falls forever downwards
Into the night sky's stardust below us.

...

I was your shining knight.
You, my damsel, riding pillion.

Through midnight hours of darkness,
Through dotted skies of stars,
Through a universe of dreams,

We were just two of pillow-touched minions.

Silver bunting crossed the sky.
We heard choirs of angels sing,
And the stars were a champagne celebration,

Through our dreams, with one million wings.

...

And our next bow on the blue spruce tree,
Is when you will so marry me.

Tudor roses and love edelweiss,
Fragrance our bed, as I make you my wife.

The Day

Lilac is the ribbon for your flowers,
Furled, looped and tied to the occasion.
Around stems of green,
Holding red roses true,
Edelweiss kisses,
The wedding posey for two.

Embroidered is your many pearls smile,
Lashes, curled, that flirt our celebration.
Diamonds to your ears,
Love heart to your chest,
Arches to your cheeks,
My bride of very best.

Black closed-toe stiletto,
Strapped buckle to ankle,

And eyes that giveth love,
The same glow, when we met.
The smile of confidence
That has grown through years.
Now is your true time to shine.

The congregation will bow and curtsy,
Your mind must pirouette show of beauty,
With bouquet outstretched on open hand,
Blossom will fall as a red petal trail of love.

This day, you truly become mine.

Chandeliers will light every step,
Crystal, hanging bowls of heaven teardrops.
A million kisses
Will tinkle in the air.
Love piano plays,
You approach, my hand flared.

There's a glisten to your love eyes,
Sparkling, are magnify glasses of your mind,
With one hundred thoughts,
A glinting to my smile.
Love piano plays,
This our moment, so shared.

Patent leather polished shoe,
Silver links, double cuff.

My eyes giveth a glance,
The glance of our own love.
And a smile that goes on forever,
Of this, our memory day.

To each other, our eyes meet.

And behold the silence of sentiment.

A pause where the world actually stops.

Every gaze forward to the couple.

The words to have an ever-meaning.

This day, ... we truly, both do shine.

Red Tudor roses and kissed edelweiss,
Fragrant our lives, ... as our hearts combine.

The Wedding Gift

The bouquet lying to your grave,
Is sentiment, you have shared our day.

For you now have a new daughter,
Who has taken our family's name.

We stand, rings on hands.

We stand in our silence.

And cry the most ever tears ...

Not of the greatest joy,
That you'd expect ...

But those, ... because you're not here.

Our love bond, silken-tied,
Shows you are not forgotten.
So, we look to the skies
And think of you,
... Hoping you have freedom.

Freedom, to have another life,
Freedom
Beyond the ribbon-tailed kite.

...

Beyond the most pain, you've
Found your own nirvana,

Far beyond our family church,
Where winged angels fly behind.

...

Our hundred is ever a million poppies ...

Thank you

Written between November 2018 and November 2019